Foundations of Programming

Philosophy, Methods and Structure

by
Mike James

I/O Press
23 Victoria Road,
Richmond, North Yorkshire, DL10 4AS

First Published 1989
©I/O Press
ISBN 1 871962 04 8

A CIP record for this book is available from the British Library

All Rights Reserved. No part of this publication may be reproduced, stored in a retrieval system, or transmitted in any form or by any means, electronic, mechanical, photocopying, recording or otherwise, without prior written permission.

Products mentioned within this text may be protected by trade marks, in which case full acknowledgement is hereby given.

Typeset by I/O Press
Printed and bound in Great Britain by Billing & Sons Ltd, Worcester.

Contents

Chapter 1	The process of programming	1
Chapter 2	The structure of control	19
Chapter 3	Modular programming	43
Chapter 4	The hierarchy	69
Chapter 5	Data = type + structure	83
Chapter 6	Formal programming methods	115
Chapter 7	Recursion	141
Chapter 8	In Von Neumann's grasp	159
Chapter 9	The art of testing and debugging	175
Further reading		185
Index		186

Preface

Many programmers are under the impression that knowing and using a particular language is all that there is to programming. In other words they feel that knowing about the latest ideas in Modula 2, Ada, C++, etc. is all there is to it. For this reason arguments between programmers tend to concentrate on which language is better than another. In practice even programmers using the same language tend to display styles that are so different that they might as well be using a completely different language. So for example, you can write Ada programs using a style that is more common in Fortran or Pascal or Cobol etc..

We have plenty of historical evidence that it is not enough to just present the new features of a language and expect programmers to understand what they are for and how to use them. This is rather like giving untrained mechanics a set of tools and expecting them to work out how to build a car - clearly many a spanner would be used as a hammer! If you agree that this is an inappropriate approach then it is worth pointing out that most programming books and courses deal with how to use a particular language and in most cases you can't see the principles for the programs. It is important that programmers learn and understand what it is they are trying to do in a way that is independent of language. This is the only way that the facilities that are offered by different languages can be evaluated and used properly.

In this book I describe how programming ideas have developed to date and outline the directions that we seem to be moving in. The topics covered include structured programming, modular programming, stepwise refinement, data flow design, Jackson structured programming, object oriented programming and design, and many others. In each case the intent has not been to explain the topic as the solution to all our ills but to throw some light on the nature of programming. In short my objective has been to give any practising programmer a better idea of what they are doing and provide some food for thought. By the time you have finished reading this book you will use your favourite language differently and you will understand why.

I realise that in writing this book I am going to upset programmers with a vested interest in any method or language that I point out as even slightly inadequate. The only thing I can say in my defence is that I have tried to spread my criticisms as widely as possible.

Mike James
September 198

Chapter One
The process of programming

Over the years of teaching people to program I have become more and more convinced that the mind of a programmer is wired differently from that of normal mortals. I am not suggesting that this is a difference that people are born with. In fact I have seen the way people think change as the result of learning to program. I have also come across a very small proportion of people who never get off the starting blocks where programming is concerned and an equally small number who are 'naturals'. What has fascinated me over the years is the way programmers think and the way that we construct programs - or rather the way we should construct programs.

This book is about programming. You might suppose that to find anything of interest here you would have to be an expert programmer - but not so. If you have any contact with computers at all then you will have some insight into what goes on. If you have worked with an 'open ended' applications package such as a spreadsheet then you will have an even better idea. If you are a programmer then you might be worried about what language will be used in this book. The answer is that, as far as possible, it will be language independent - there are issues of programming that go beyond considerations of which language is used to express our thoughts. Of course there is a great deal of practical value in understanding features that make one language better, or rather more appropriate for a particular job and most of the ideas are illustrated with examples from many programming languages.

The process is the program

It is often said that precision and logic are the prime characteristics of programming and programmers. I think that the truth is slightly different. What characterises the way that the current generation of programmers think is **process**. A program is a list of instructions that is obeyed by a computer. It is a list of instructions that tells the computer what to do and in this sense it is a static representation of something dynamic. On the face of it a program appears to be just something written on paper like any other piece of text. It isn't. To a casual observer its most distinctive characteristics are the unfamiliar words and perhaps layout. This causes many a non-programmer to assume that the key to understanding programs is just learning the hidden code. But a program is far from just a familiar idea wrapped up in a foreign language.

In a sense a program is a detailed description of a mechanism that 'comes to life' when it is obeyed by a computer. In most branches of engineering a mechanism is described using drawings and specifications and then a human builds whatever it is. The human is usually intelligent and skilled at the job and so the result is the product of a process of interpretation. The mechanism usually works because the people realising it make it so. For example, if you are building a house from a set of plans and written specifications it is assumed that you know how to lay bricks and make a waterproof roof. In the case of a program however a computer is responsible for implementation - and we all know that they lack intelligence and skill! For this reason a program has to be an exact specification of what happens.

To understand the true nature of a program it is perhaps better to think about a plan of a machine that moves rather than of something static like a house. When you look at a house plan your only problem is generally in thinking it into 3D and most people can manage this. However when you look at the plan of an engine then, even if you can imagine it in 3D, it is much harder to imagine how the pieces move. A static plan cannot convey movement and it is up to you to animate it in your imagination.

The same is true of a static list of instructions. To the non-programmer the text is stationary and appears just like any other prose but to the programmer the text is pure movement! Seeing movement in a diagram is a skill that makes an engineer and seeing the process captured in a program is the skill that makes a programmer.

What makes a program?

If the raw stuff of programming is a list of instructions, then the place to start an investigation of programming is to examine the types of behaviour exhibited by a general list of instructions. The simplest form any list of instructions can take is a 'one after the other arrangement'. This is the type of list that everyone is used to. They tell you how to make a pie, operate a video recorder, assemble a model kit and all manner of ordinary things. Placing instructions one after the other in this way is generally referred to as **sequencing**.

The first programs that you learn to write are like this but you quickly run out of interesting problems that can be tackled at this level. Most beginners are quickly introduced to the additional features of loops and selection and then spend the rest of their lives trying to master them!

Selection is simply the ability to vary the instructions according to the conditions. For example, a set of instructions to operate a video recorder could start with "IF you have model 1 THEN ignore steps 20 through 40". A **loop** is simply the ability to repeat a portion of the instructions until some condition or result is achieved. It is more difficult to come up with clear examples of loops in lists that are not programs because they are usually hidden in vague English descriptions. For example, the instructions for putting together a model aeroplane might say "wait until the glue dries". It would be unusual to find this expressed in its full form of

1. do something else for 30 mins
2. check if the glue is dry
3. if glue isn't dry go back to 1.
4. continue with the assembly

but that's what actually happens. Most of the repetitions in everyday life are hidden in this way. This is perhaps what makes it difficult for novice programmers to actually get to grips with loops and make them explicit. Novice programmers genuinely have difficulty seeing that a process is a repetition at all. When they do notice that something is being repeated they then have difficulty translating this into a description of what is being repeated! This manifests itself as apparently trivial errors such as leaving statements outside the loop that should be inside, forgetting to finish the loop, misidentifying the start of the loop etc.. These errors look very foolish and even a slightly experienced programmer finds difficult to imagine making the same mistakes. If you are involved in teaching programming, it is worth remembering that such errors are not evidence of a sloppy approach but are due to the lack of an ability to perceive the standard flow of control. It takes time to build up the mental models of process that makes the difference between programmer and non-programmer.

Atomic theory

At this point we have a definition of a program as a list of instructions that are obeyed one after another in sequence, selected depending on the condition, and repeated. That really is all there is to it. All the programs that have ever been written, or can be written, are composed of nothing but selection and repetition. Not only that but if you go on a search for anything different in real lists of instructions you won't find anything different. Sequencing, selection and looping are the basic atoms that make up every list of instructions and hence every program.

In the early days of programming this truth must have been known but it didn't really make much impression on programming practice. Although selection and repetition are just two categories, there are an almost infinite number of variations on these simple themes. The early programming languages didn't provide these forms as single commands. Instead you had to create them out of smaller instructions such as the GOTO, JMP or BRA command. This allowed a great deal of freedom in how loops and selects could be created and this obscured their fundamental nature. If loops and selects are the atoms of programming then you could say that instructions like GOTO are the subatomic particles.

It took until the '60s and the invention of **structured programming** for us to realise that restricting the freedom of expression within programs to a small number of types of selection and loops was a good thing. Structured programming was one of the first **programming methods** to result from people thinking about the process of programming. There have been plenty of others since and some of these are covered in Chapter Six.

All programming methods are concerned with how we do or should program but they sometimes differ in their intent. Originally structured programming was intended to **de-skill** programming and make programmers out of non-programmers without having to invest in a great deal of training. As it turned out, the philosophical content of structured programming is of more interest to skilled programmers than the de-skilled! In practice there are no rigorous programming methods that are guaranteed to produce good programs without the help of human creativity and judgment. If there were machines could take over their own programming! Currently programming methods are just guidelines that help us in our task. We have no even vaguely complete or rigorous theory of programming.

The goal

You may at this point be wondering what more there is to say about programming? Programming sounds simple, just a matter of describing what happens in sufficient detail for a machine to perform the desired task. This is indeed one view of programming and it was dominant in the early days. Programming is a very young craft and it is unique in having to cope with an amazing rate of improvement in its basic tools. In one (human) generation computers have gone from machines that filled a room but only offered the power of today's pocket calculators to desktop machines that only a few years ago would have been described as supercomputers. Back in the early days the objectives were to get the expensive machine to do the job and about the only requirements were that the program worked, and worked in a time that was affordable. It was almost as if the task of programming itself was such an effort that there was nothing left over to look at what we were actually doing. Programmer - programmer interaction was at the level of swapping clever tricks and it was very rare that anyone thought to discuss the programs themselves. The reason was that any informed discussion had to be about how to do things such as sort a list into order, calculate some result or how best to display results to users. Programming was so new that many of the standard methods or algorithms that we now take for granted still had to be invented.

As things moved on the emphasis shifted from how to do something to how best to write it down. It's almost as if having mastered writing we are now free to concentrate on style. Of course this still begs the question of why we should even consider style? The reason is that as well as being for the machine to execute, programs are for programmers to read. If you have two correct programs one written in a bad style and one written in a good style then roughly speaking a machine will have no difficulty in obeying either. When it comes to a human however it is a very different story. The program written in a bad style will be difficult to understand and it might even be impossible to achieve a complete understanding of it. If you don't understand a program then there is no hope that you will be able to modify or extend it with any confidence. In fact if the program is that difficult to understand the chances are that the programmer who created it will also not have understood it and hence if it works it is more due to luck than skill. Now it is not enough that a program works it also has to be a clear expression of what the program does. Paradoxically increasing the clarity of a program also increases the chances that it will work so in this sense we are still satisfying the original need!

The main objection to the idea of writing a clear program is efficiency. It is very often said that it is worth sacrificing clarity if some trick will deliver a performance increase. This is sometimes true but it isn't an argument against modern programming methods rather a comment on the quality of our current hardware. Even if you do need to use a dirty trick to make a program practical on a particular machine you can still write the vast bulk of the program in a good style and add copious comments around the section that is mucky in an attempt to explain what is happening.

All that remains is to explore the nature of programming to discover how processes can be most clearly represented in static text.

The flow of control

If you are reading, or in the computer's case, obeying, a list of instructions then you will follow a definite course through the list. (If not you are a broken computer randomly executing instructions!) It is possible to imagine all the possible courses through a program drawn out as a sort of road map. This 'road map' or **flow of control graph** gives you a better idea of the dynamic nature of a program than just the static text and it also seems to correspond to something real in every programmer's mind. What the theory behind structured programming tell us is that this road map is made up of three basic shapes:

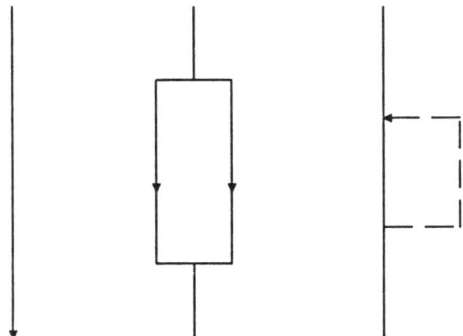

The diagram for selection suggests that a choice is made between two alternatives and the loop literally 'loops back' on itself to achieve repetition. There are other ways to achieve selection and repetition but these shapes do seem to correspond to the basic units that many programmers use to construct programs. For example, if you watch a programmer reading a program you will very often see hand movements that sketch out a circle every time a loop is encountered. This is a programmer's habit that mimics the action of the program and it is rather like mouthing the sound that each letter makes as you read!

As these are the basic shapes that make up any program clarity of expression should be linked to how easy it is to represent these in the text of a program.

The text and the dynamic

The shapes used to describe the flow of control in a program emphasise the fact that the dynamic form of a program doesn't correspond to the text layout on the page. For example, most programming languages allow you to make selections using a statement along the lines of:

>   IF *condition* THEN
>   *list1*
>   ELSE
>   *list2*
>   ENDIF

where *list1* and *list2* are two alternative lists of instructions. Even in the most limited sense you can see that the layout of the program doesn't correspond to the flow of control diagram given above. At best it is a mangled version of the flow of control graph forced to conform to our top to bottom left to right reading habits. Many beginners get confused about what happens if the route through *list1* is followed - is *list2* obeyed? The answer is, of course, that *list2* is skipped if *list1* is obeyed and vice versa but you should be able to see the scope for confusion. The reason for the difficulty is that *list2* is written directly below *list1* and by the natural flow of control this means it should be obeyed. In many ways a more natural layout would be:

>   *first part*
>   *of program*
>   IF *condition*
>   THEN   ELSE
>   ..   ..
>   *list 1*   *list 2*
>   ..   ..
>   ENDIF
>   *remainder of*
>   *program*

I'm not suggesting that we should adopt this form of layout, in most languages it isn't even possible, but every skilled programmer seems to transform IF..THEN..ELSE statements into this form without even being aware of it. One of the causes of the difficulty in programming is the very restricted form of text layout that is acceptable. The natural shape of the flow of control graph has to be squashed into a single column of instructions that reads naturally or unnaturally depending on your point of view from left to right.

It is interesting to note that spreadsheet programming does provide the freedom to lay out programs in more than a left to right top to bottom mode. When you write a program within a spreadsheet the instructions have to be placed in a column and then they are obeyed one after another top to bottom. As a typical spreadsheet contains more than 100 columns you can see that there is scope for creative layout. In particular when the flow of control divides into two paths this could be made more evident by using two new columns. For example,

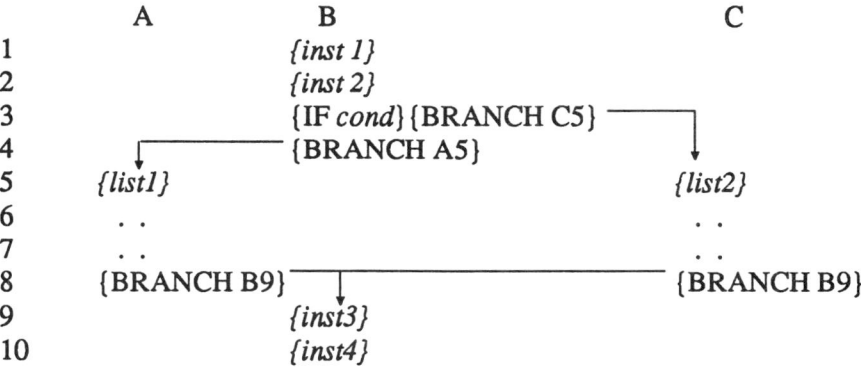

executes the list of instructions in column C if the condition is true and the list of instructions in column A otherwise. The clarity of this example is spoiled by the fact the most spreadsheet languages only provide a primitive IF command and this means that you have to use a lot of BRANCH instructions to make up for it. In principle however there is no reason why the instruction {IF *cond*} shouldn't transfer control to the column to the right if *cond* is true and to the left if false and this might make the structure clear.

The difficult case of the loop

In the case of a loop the discrepancy between what is written and the dynamic form is even greater. For example, many modern languages have a statement to create loops along the lines of:

> DO
> *list to be repeated*
> LOOP

The words DO and LOOP can be thought of as forming brackets around the list of statements that are to be repeated. Of course as written this results in an infinite loop. A simple way of indicating when the loop should end is to write the finishing condition alongside the DO or the LOOP statement. For example,

> DO
> PRINT hello
> LOOP until 3 times round

In this form even the image of a loop is hidden. What loops back and to where? If you come from a slightly older school of programming - assembler, Fortran etc.. then you might be translating this more modern form of loop into something like:

> x:
> PRINT hello
> GOTO x

where x: is a label that marks a point in the program. In this form you can see the action of looping back more clearly - the GOTO (JMP or BRA in assembler) command transfers control back to the point marked x:

> x: ←──────┐
> PRINT hello │
> GOTO x ─────┘

The use of a label such as x to mark a point in a program that another instruction can refer to has virtually been abandoned. It was *the* way of dealing with the problem of selecting between alternatives and constructing loops but, as will be explained, it is so open to misuse that it has been replaced. This is in the main good but these replacements are further from the real action of a program and so more abstract.

If you think I'm making a fuss about nothing consider the following simple question about the FOR loop. Most computer languages have a construct similar to a FOR loop that can be used to repeat a block of instructions a given number of times. For example,

>   FOR i=1 TO 3
>   PRINT "hello"
>   NEXT i

will repeat the PRINT statement three times - that is 'for values of i from 1 to 3'. This is just as abstract a way of writing a loop as the DO..LOOP and once again there is no real suggestion of the action of looping back. Even so most novice programmers do conceive of the FOR loop in terms of looping, the NEXT i statement causing a loop back to the line containing the word FOR. There is no problem with this until you ask yourself what

>   i=1
>   FOR i= i TO i+2
>   PRINT "hello"
>   NEXT i

means? If the loop back is to the FOR statement then surely the start and finish values will vary - when the loop is first encountered i will be 1 and the FOR statement is FOR i=1 TO 3, after the first loop back i is 2 the FOR statement is FOR i=2 TO 4 and so on.. Clearly in this case the loop never ends. Almost any programmer will tell you that this is not the way that FOR loops work. The usual explanation is that the start and finish values in a FOR loop are evaluated once at the start of the loop and then stored in 'some other place' so that they remain fixed. However another way of looking at this is that the NEXT i statement causes a loop back to the statement just following the FOR statement. In other words, the loop starts just inside where most programmers think it does!

If you think that this example is too extreme to be taken seriously consider a simpler question. In the loop

```
FOR i=2 TO 1
   PRINT "hello"
NEXT i
```

do you see the word "hello" printed? The FOR loop is supposed to end when the value of i is greater than the final value but in this case it starts out bigger than the final value. The answer is that it all depends on where the test is carried out, at the beginning of the loop or at the end and this differs from language to language. In the jargon, it all depends on whether it is a WHILE FOR or an UNTIL FOR and this isn't evident simply from the way the FOR loop is written.

All of this goes to demonstrate that in the case of loops the way that we write them has little to do with the dynamic behaviour that they produce. Just as in the case of the IF statement, I am not suggesting that the way loops are written should be changed to reflect more accurately what they cause to happen. I am just trying to highlight the fact that the connection between the text of a program and the action of a program is rather subtle and getting more so as programming languages develop.

Making the best of it

The whole question of how the text of a program relates to its structure is a very important one but apart from inventing your own new language there isn't much you can do to improve the situation. This makes the few methods that are available to make the structure in an existing language more visible well worth using.

The best known such method is **indenting**. The basic idea is to use layout to mark blocks of instructions as distinct paragraphs in the program. For example, the simple two way selection IF..THEN..ELSE can be laid out as:

```
IF a=0 THEN PRINT "a is zero" ELSE PRINT "a isn't zero"
```

or

```
IF a=0 THEN
PRINT "a is zero"
ELSE
PRINT "a isn't zero"
ENDIF
```

but it is much easier to see where each group of instructions starts and stops in

```
IF a=0 THEN
    PRINT "a is zero"
ELSE
    PRINT "a isn't zero"
ENDIF
```

In the same way the body of a loop should be indented to make the distinction between what is repeated and what controls the repetition. For example,

```
DO
    PRINT "hello"
    INPUT a
LOOP UNTIL a=0
```

Indenting is a crude but essential graphical method of marking out the different sections of a program. Perhaps as our technology improves we will be able to adopt conventions such as using a different type face or font to mark the structure of a program. For example,

IF a=0 **THEN**
    PRINT "a is zero"
ELSE
    PRINT "a isn't zero"
ENDIF

When such typographical control isn't available the same sort of layout effect can be achieved using upper and lower case as in

>   IF a=0 THEN
>   print "a is zero"
>   ELSE
>   print "a isn't zero"
>   ENDIF

The whole subject of layout is a contentious one and very much a matter for personal taste but you should always strive for a layout that reveals rather than hides the program's structure.

The power of looping

Although programming starts to become interesting once you introduce ways of making a selection, it really only becomes powerful once you can construct a loop. Without a loop a program can only run for a time that is directly proportional to the number of instructions you are prepared to write. In practical terms this means that without loops no program would last longer than a few seconds! It is only by using loops to repeat sections of code in conjunction with IF statements to vary what happens according to the prevailing conditions that any of our large scale programs such as word processors etc. are possible.

Another consequence of the power of a loop is that the time that a machine spends obeying any part of a program isn't proportional to the number of instructions it contains. The old advice to look at the contents of loops if you are trying to optimise a program is based on the observation that a program spends most of its machine time in loops. A rather more clear statement of this is in the equally old saying that a program spends 90% of its time in 10% of its instructions. It is important for every programmer to try to dissociate the length of a section of the program text from the time that it occupies the computer.

Capturing process-a blind alley?

So programming is about capturing the way things happen or should happen in a static description. The text of a program is a snapshot of a process and this is what makes a program different from most other forms of written material. The order in which the instructions are obeyed create within the program a line or track along which time progresses. As the instructions are obeyed the unmoving program is animated to create a working mechanism.

This may be the essence of a program but almost since the first moment programming came into being we have been trying to escape the limitations of expressing processes as static text. There are so many limitations it is difficult to know where to begin but perhaps the most obvious and the most vital leads us to the **Von Neumann** bottleneck. The whole concept of a program and the flow of control depends upon an assumption that the processor will obey one instruction at a time.

If you remove this restriction in an attempt to make things go faster and allow more than one computer loose on the same program at the same time then the result is chaos. If it is difficult to capture a process that involves one active agent in a piece of static text then it is very difficult to manage the same trick if two active agents are involved. You can attempt to invent ways around the problem by assigning different portions of the text to each processor and provide ways that the two can interact but this doesn't seem to make the problem any easier for the mind to grasp.

The reason is that while we can cope with the idea of animating a single piece of static text, animating and coordinating more than one is the stuff of nervous breakdowns. It can be done but it is hard work and error prone. Much work is currently going on into ways of automatically splitting programs down into portions that can be executed in parallel and as we approach the speed limit of a single processor this work is becoming increasingly urgent! Some of the technicalities of concurrent programming are described in Chapter Eight.

Is there another way?

It is usually assumed that the single processor Von Neumann bottleneck is a hardware problem, but you should now be able to see that it is a simple consequence of the nature of programs. This raises the question of whether or not there is an alternative way of capturing and specifying processes without using text. At the moment the answer is no but there are some moves in that direction with **object-oriented programming**.

A totally different approach to the problem is to try to avoid the concept of a process at all. Traditional programs, the ones that attempt to capture the essence of a process, are generally referred to as **procedural** (not to be confused with the use of the word procedure to mean module or subroutine). So to avoid the Von Neumann bottleneck what we need is a **non-procedural** approach to programming.

This may sound mad but it is in fact the easiest and most natural way of introducing parallelism into computing. It is however one that many programmers see as primitive, or even fail to see at all. A question is probably the best way of illustrating the idea. Describe how you would add up a column of figures? If you are a programmer then you are almost certainly already thinking about loops like:

```
i=1
DO
   get number i
   add number i to total
   increment i
LOOP until last number added
```

This may not be the way that you choose to express your loop but it captures the basic idea of adding each number in turn to a total - it is also clearly a process. Now if you set any spreadsheet user the same problem you will get a quite different answer. A spreadsheet user will tell you that there is no 'process' of adding up the column of numbers. Each number is present in a separate cell and the total is just a formula entered into another cell - namely SUM(column). The relationship between the column of numbers and the formula SUM(column) is kept true at all times by the spreadsheet. As new values are entered the formula is recalculated but the user can be blissfully unaware of this. As far as they are concerned how the formula continues to show the current sum is irrelevant - it just does. Notice that there is no suggestion of a process here. In theory a spreadsheet is a static relationship of data and equations. So one man's process is another's static spreadsheet! If you allocate one processor per spreadsheet cell then you have a parallel computer that avoids nearly all of the problems of traditional programming. In this sense the spreadsheet may be a million miles from advanced programming but it is one view of the future none the less. If you find spreadsheets too demeaning then you can find the same approach of converting process into static relationships in a more traditional language-based form in Prolog, logic and declarative programming.

A general skill

What have we learned about programming and programmers? I suppose you could say that the main idea is that programmers are concerned with describing activities. Most non-programmers are familiar with using language to describe objects but not activities in the detail required to create a program. Programmers do seem to have the atoms of any process - selection and looping - built into their heads. This enables them to see complex processes for what they are and represent them in a static written form without too much effort. This isn't the whole story but it goes some of the way to explaining how we program and why we fail. It also explains why some people are of the opinion that programming is a general skill that should be taught to administrators, managers, politicians etc., present and future, as a way of improving the way that they solve problems. How is it possible to cope in the modern world without such skills? - It isn't.

key points

- Programming is the art of capturing dynamic processes in static text.

- The basic control structures of all dynamic processes are sequencing, selection and looping.

- Programmers can identify these basic structures in processes and use this to write accurate descriptions of said processes.

- There should be a direct and easy to see relationship between the program's text and the basic control structures.

- Typography and layout should be used to make the dynamic structure of a program more evident in a program's text.

- Non-procedural programming may become possible in the future by defining relationships between data and allowing the computer to find its own ways of maintaining them.

- Programming is a general skill that should be taught to all.

Chapter Two
The structure of control

Structured programming is one of the best known programming method, and is the most misunderstood. The microcomputer revolution which began over ten years ago now, introduced more people to programming than ever before but in many cases it was a very rough and ready education. I'm not being critical of self-taught programmers nor am I being elitist - many Polytechnic and University trained programmers make it through their course without ever understanding anything of the deeper aspects of programming. What I am concerned about is that programmers should keep an open mind and interest in their subject. You may have learned BASIC on a PC or Pascal on a Cray supercomputer, but unless you look beyond the almost routine task of coding instructions to the way that you create programs, you will never develop as a programmer.

The trouble with this platitude is that if you just think about programming you are almost certain to favour the way that you currently program. In other words, you tend to favour any philosophy that backs up the way that you are currently working and argue violently with anything that suggests otherwise! Every article I have ever written, or lecture that I have given, introducing any sort of programming method has met with objections from the non-believers and believers alike. The non-believers mostly complain that the ideas are too rigid and restrictive and stifle their creative urges. The believers generally complain that my version of 'The Method' is far too weak and the non-believers should be MADE to program correctly, not just cajoled into it.

Coders <> programmers

This polarisation is made worse by the history of structured programming and the view that many computer 'professionals' have of programmers. Back in the early days of computing there was a shortage of good programmers - there always has been and some dare to suggest that there always will be! To make a little expertise go further the people who knew about computers were removed from the job of actually writing programs. Instead they designed overall plans of what should happen and a technician converted these plans into actual program code. The creators were often called **'analysts'** and the coders were called 'programmers' in their job descriptions but were still thought of as 'coders'.

It was generally thought or hoped that the skilled part of the job was confined to the analysts and the programmers were the computer manual labourers. Even so there still weren't enough manual labourers to go around and something had to be done. The answer seemed to be to find a way of de-skilling programming to the point where a reasonably trained monkey could do the job. As a result lots of programmers were taught programming methods as a set of inflexible rules that attempted to ensure that they could do the job correctly but without much understanding. Of course the endeavour failed because good coding requires a lot of understanding.

The new hacker

We are just leaving an era of programming where the hardware was dominant. Even now programmers are occasionally forced to leave the cosy world of high level languages and deal with assembler for some tasks. But it's only a matter of a few years ago that any real computer application demanded assembly language. When Bill Gates wrote the first Microsoft BASIC he didn't use C or any sort of high level language, it was pure machine code. By this I mean that, rather than just writing the program in logically correct assembly language, Bill Gates used his knowledge of the microprocessor hardware to select particular instructions that saved memory or took less time. If you have ever tried this sort of programming you will know that it has its own fascination and reward. I too have spent hours altering otherwise perfectly correct code just to improve its performance!

The same sort of attitude could be found in the early days of languages such as Fortran and BASIC. When you first learned the language no mention was made of how to make things go faster, all that mattered was producing a logically correct program. Once you had used the language you soon added to your knowledge a collection of rules about how to write an efficient program. For example, use FOR loops in preference to any other type of loop, omit the variable from NEXT statements, use integer variables wherever possible, combine instructions on a single line etc.. None of these recommendations have anything to do with the logic of the program. Indeed many of them make a program dense and difficult to follow, so obscuring the logic.

This sort of hardware-oriented programming is undeniably clever and its practitioners are very skilled. The trouble is that the programs that result are beasts that give their obedience to only one person - their creator. While this may satisfy the megalomaniac in all of us it isn't a good basis for producing a commercial product. Many companies have suffered because they employed someone who had sufficient grasp of the hardware to make the computer sit up and beg, jump through hoops of fire and generally impress everyone. Impressive though this is at the time, the reckoning usually comes when the person in question moves on to the next interesting job - leaving behind a program that is beyond any mortal's understanding. Such programs also have a habit of failing in spectacular ways. Because they often exploit undocumented features or stretch the hardware and systems software to the limit, they usually succeed in taking it beyond breaking point. These are the errors of completely catastrophic failure. They generally bring the whole system to a halt with no simple way of recovery and no hope of ever finding out why it happened. I suppose in the world of engineering this is rather like a mechanic building a custom car that only *he* understands and can make work. Custom cars can be fun but putting one into mass production would be a contradiction.

Spaghetti code

There is another type of programming that has nothing to be said for it at all and yet it can be difficult to distinguish from the intelligent use of system characteristics. If you modify a program away from its most logical form to achieve an improvement in performance then you are paying a price for something that you want. On the other hand if you write a program that is overly complex just because you cannot be bothered to write it any other way then you are paying a price for nothing. Some programmers are taught by having the workings of each instruction in the language explained without any guidance about how they should be used to create programs. This is rather like showing a mechanic a box of tools and expecting him to work out what everything is used for. Of course some mechanics would know what to do with a spanner but you would still find much misuse! In the case of programming the misuse takes the form of control statements doing jobs they were never meant for. The best example of this is the careless use of the direct transfer instruction - GOTO in BASIC and Fortran, JMP or BRA in most assembly languages- which transfers control to a labelled point in the program.

As described in Chapter One direct transfer instructions are intended to form loops and IF statements. A transfer to a point earlier in a program should be a loop and a transfer forward is either due to getting out of a loop or making a selection. Fine in theory but if you introduce the GOTO statement as "GOTO 100 transfers control to line 100" and that's all you have got to say about it then you can expect it to be misused. In practice you will see the GOTO, JMP or BRA instruction used for jumping about in a program any way that suits the moment. This is sometimes called opportunistic programming because, rather than plan ahead, the programmer just makes use of any convenient section of code by jumping to it. The result is a flow of control graph (a diagram of all the possible paths through a program) that resembles a bowl of spaghetti and hence the less kind label of "spaghetti programming" has been added to the jargon. Spaghetti code is bad because an overly complex program has little chance of being understood and that includes by its creator. A program that isn't completely understood is almost certain to contain bugs.

The good, the not too bad and the very ugly

Structured programming, and all programming methods, attempt to show how programs can be written such that their logic is clear to any reader. A good programmer writes programs for other programmers to read. A machine coder writes programs mainly for machines and a spaghetti coder write programs for themselves alone. The basic principle of structured programming is to use only a small number of types of loop and IF statements to construct programs and to use them in a way that reflects the inner logic of the program. Some computer languages are said to be structured because they provide WHILE, UNTIL and FOR loops and IF..THEN..ELSE statements. This has caused many programmers to think that it is the language which has to be structured not the programmer! It *is* possible to write structured programs in any language - even assembler.

A good programmer will attempt to build programs using the most appropriate loops and selections to suit the situation. A not too bad programmer will be prepared to modify this ideal structure to gain some necessary, but not gratuitous, performance improvement. The truly bad programmer will never have heard or thought about any of these ideas and will produce very ugly programs indeed.

The loop family

The idea that selection and looping were the basic building blocks of all programming was introduced in Chapter One. Most programmers are agreed that the IF..THEN..ELSE statement is about as good as any other form of selection statement. Hence most high level languages have some variety of IF..THEN..ELSE statement. What they are not so agreed on is the types of loop that should be provided. They all more or less agree that there should be a FOR loop - but when it comes to other types of conditional loops they diverge.

A FOR, or enumeration, loop is a special sort of loop where you know how many times the repeat should be performed. This should be contrasted to a true conditional loop where you have to keep on testing for the exit condition each time round the loop. For example, if you want to print HELLO five times then you know how many times to go around the loop before it starts and so this can be written as a FOR loop

> FOR i=1 TO 5
>   PRINT "HELLO"
> NEXT i

However if you are reading in values from a user until they type a particular value, -1 say, then you have no idea how many times you need to go around the loop and this needs a true conditional loop. There are many different ways of writing a conditional loop but most programmers would understand

> DO
>   INPUT a
> LOOP UNTIL a=-1

There is no simple or clear way of converting this loop into a FOR loop. Even if you do succeed in finding a way of doing it the point is that you don't want to! The first loop is an enumeration loop and as such it suits a FOR loop and this isn't true of the second loop. If you find that you are using nothing but FOR loops then it is time to examine your programming style. Most loops are enumeration loops but there is a hard core of loops that cannot be written as FOR loops.

Conditional loops

It has already been mentioned that older languages expected programmers to construct whatever type of conditional loop they needed using GOTO instructions. As programming developed it was recognised that it would be simpler to provide language facilities that implemented the loops that were being created using GOTO instructions as purpose built instructions. Languages that had such advanced commands were often referred to as structured languages although this is something of a misnomer as only programs can be structured; languages merely provide facilities that either help or hinder in this aim.

The language Pascal was one of the first popular structured languages and it provided two types of conditional loop - WHILE and UNTIL. As a result many programmers claim that these are the only types of loop that should be used to create structured programs. This is far from true and in fact Pascal's (and other languages!) WHILE and UNTIL loops are very poor because they manage to mix up two important concepts - exit position and exit sense. Exit position is simply the placement of the exit point within the loop. The WHILE loop has its exit point at the start of the loop whereas the UNTIL loop has its exit point at the end. The practical effect of placing the exit point in different positions is that the action of the WHILE loop can be skipped but the action of the UNTIL loop has to be performed at least once. This is often said as " a WHILE loop can go round zero times but an UNTIL loop must go round once". In Pascal there is another difference between the two forms of loop. The condition specified in the WHILE loop has to be false to exit the loop but in the UNTIL loop it has to be true to exit. In other words the sense of the exit condition is different.

In a simple form of language the WHILE loop is

>   xxx: IF NOT *condition* THEN exit loop
>   *loop action*
>   GOTO xxx

and the UNTIL loop is

>   xxx: *loop action*
>   IF *condition* THEN exit loop
>   GOTO xxx

Shifting the exit position and altering the exit sense in this way is useful because it corresponds to the two most common forms of conditional loop. However, in my opinion, it does tend to confuse these two elements of loop creation. A better method can be found in a more modern language such as QuickBASIC or Turbo BASIC which allows you to form loops using the key words DO and LOOP to bracket the section of code to be repeated. Exit conditions can formed at the start or at the end of the loop and the exit sense can be specified by using the keywords WHILE or UNTIL. A WHILE exit condition has to be false for the loop to terminate and an UNTIL condition has to be true for the loop to terminate. In other

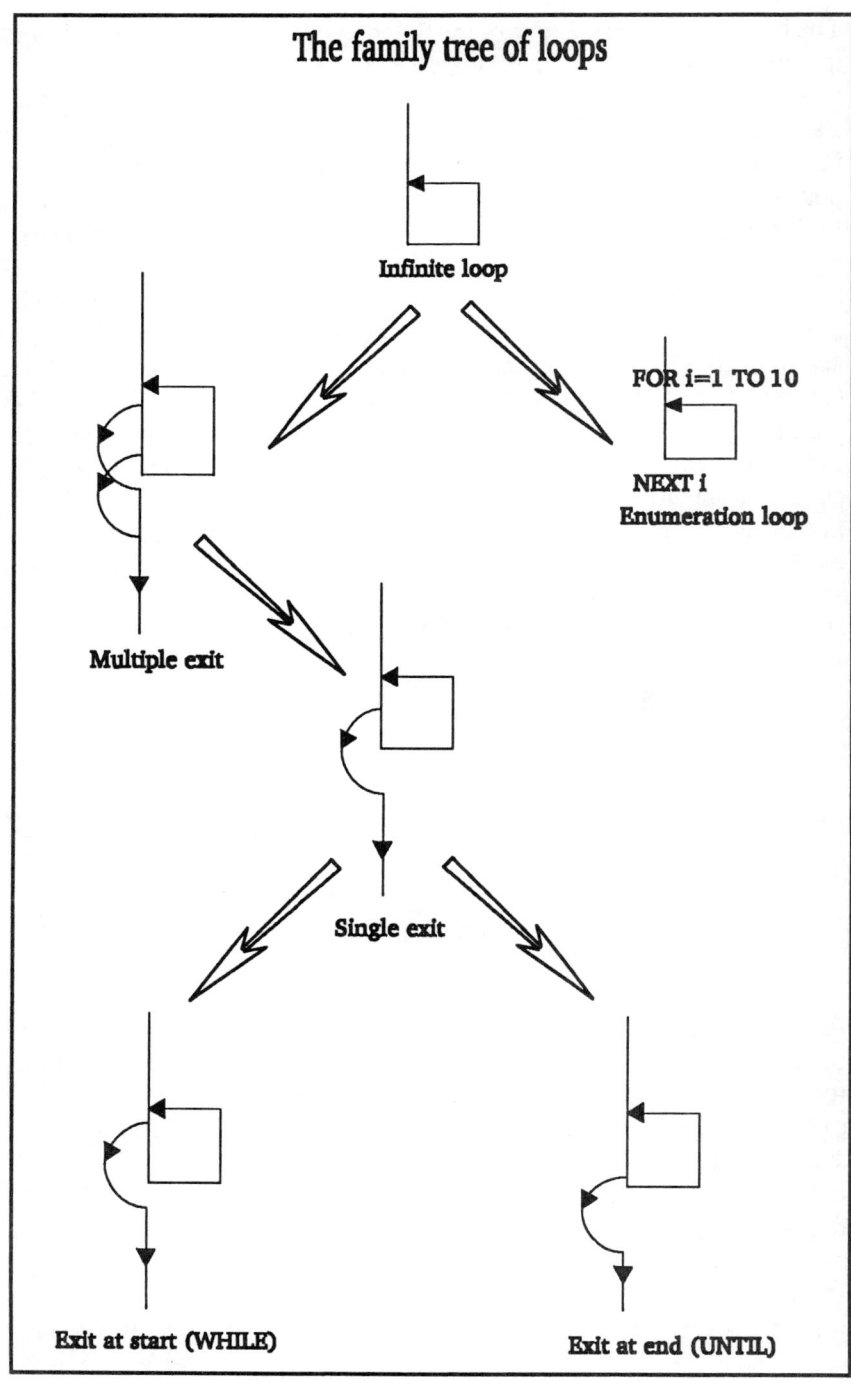

words UNTIL *condition* is equivalent to WHILE not(*condition*) and vice versa. For example, you can write a Pascal like WHILE loop as

>DO WHILE *condition*
>   *actions*
>LOOP

but you can also create a loop with a WHILE exit condition at the end of the loop

>DO
>   *actions*
>LOOP WHILE *condition*

and the *condition* has to be false for the loop to end.

When you create a loop the only real question is where the exit point should be situated. Most modern languages only allow exit points at the start and end of a loop but there is no reason why an exit point shouldn't be positioned somewhere within the body of a loop. In this case there will be some statements before the exit and some after it

>DO
>   *actions1*
>IF *condition* THEN EXIT LOOP
>   *actions2*
>LOOP

You should be able to see that the pre-exit actions will be carried out once more than the post-exit actions. In this sense you could say that such a loop goes round so many times and a bit!

The final loop complication is the possibility of multiple exit points. Almost no modern structured language allows this! The reason is loops can always be reorganised to gather together all of the exit points into one. However it is sometimes easier and logically clearer to write something like

```
            DO
               actions 1
            IF condition1 THEN EXIT LOOP
               actions 2
            IF condition2 THEN EXIT LOOP
               actions 3
            LOOP
```

Gathering all of this information together you can see that the conditional loop can be classified according to the number of exit points and their positioning. Single exit point loops are the simplest and those positioning the exit at the start or the end of the loop are particularly simple.

How particular languages realise these standard control structures is described later in this chapter.

Whose structure is it anyway?

Now we have listed all the possible basic control structures that are needed to create a program. The principle of structured programming is that we should select a small number of them and use them and only them. Languages like Pascal make the choice for you providing an IF statement, FOR loop and two single exit point conditional loops, one with a WHILE sense exit point at the start and one with an UNTIL sense exit point at the end. Programmers who equate structured programming with Pascal's selection often comment on my own use of other structures in languages such as Turbo BASIC, C or assembler. I do not advocate the level of restriction that Pascal applies to a programmer but would prefer to allow programmers freedom to choose the form that best expresses the purpose of the program. If you understand and know all the forms that a loop can take then why shouldn't you be free to choose? Of course Pascal was designed during those dark ages when programmers were never intended to understand anything and so they had to be coerced into using a small number of correct structures.

Sequencing and nesting game

Structured programming is very like building a program out of cards each one of which represents one of the possible forms - i.e. using IF, FOR, WHILE, UNTIL etc. cards. There are only two possible ways of putting these cards together - sequencing and nesting. Sequencing simply means putting one card after another to give an IF statement followed by a WHILE loop, followed by a FOR loop etc.. Nesting is a little more complicated and involve putting one card completely 'inside' another. For example, you might put one FOR loop completely within another FOR loop

>   FOR i=1 TO 10
>   FOR j=1 TO 10
>   PRINT i,j
>   NEXT j
>   NEXT i

You should be able to see that this double loop exhibits a counting behaviour that is more complex than a single loop, i.e. the j values change more quickly than the i values. In general, nesting of simple structures is the way that complex and powerful programs are created. It is the use of IF statements within loops, within IF statements within other loops, and so on, that produces interesting behaviour. Sequencing is necessary but slightly boring!

Notice that as control structures have to be completely nested within one another, this rules out conditional or unconditional jumps into or out of loops and IF statements.

Thus, in the structured view of programming, putting together a program simply involves selecting which structures to use and combining them using sequencing and nesting. Who could argue with that?

The myth of the evil GOTO

Much of the theory of programming has been confused by one simple and very common misunderstanding - that the GOTO command is in some way evil. Many programmers believe that modern programming methods state that the use of the GOTO is forbidden and if you do find yourself using it then you are a bad programmer. If you do believe this then a small logical extension results in the conclusion that languages that make heavy use of the GOTO are similarly evil. Of course this is a lot of nonsense!

Back in the early days of computers the only facilities that were provided for creating the flow of control in the program were direct and conditional jumps. In assembly language these were usually called BRA (BRAnch) or JMP (JuMP) instructions and these made their way into higher level languages as the GOTO instruction of Fortran and later BASIC. From these very primitive transfer instructions the programmer was expected to construct all of the forms of control needed within a program - the only problem was that this fact was rarely mentioned and many programmers were very bad at it! As a result the programs that were written at the time were often a mess with control being passed all over the place. Any of these programs could have been written (or even converted) into a collection of sequenced and nested loops and selects but their programmers had mangled this simple structure as they were created.

The problem with the GOTO is that it captures the essence of programming on too small a level. You can write programs by transferring control to where it is needed on an ad-hoc basis and if you do this you will find that the result is made up of loops and selects as promised. They may be hidden but they are still there! It is much better to think directly in terms of loops and selects when you construct a program and this is the reason that modern programming languages provide specific instructions for these forms and so make the GOTO virtually redundant. However if you are using a language that isn't so advanced you can still use the GOTO to produce well structured programs.

For and against

After you have been using structured programming for a while it is difficult to remember what it was like to not think explicitly in terms of loops and selection and this makes it very difficult to deal with objections to the method. Indeed in the form I have described, structured programming isn't really a method more the objective to write clear, easy to understand programs that don't rely on dirty tricks to work. There are two sorts of programmers who find that they have to be hostile to structured programming. The first has no choice but to use tricky coding to achieve some result that would be impossible otherwise. In this case there is no point in arguing - when they move on to a different programming environment the method will win them over because they clearly think about programming. The second chooses to produce unstructured programs because they claim it gives them freedom of expression or for some other ad-hoc reason. In this case there is little to be done except to explain, and explain again.

In many ways much worse than the hostiles are the belligerent supporters of structured programming, or whatever method or language is in vogue. It is not enough to tell a fellow programmer that it should be done in a particular way - you also have to explain why. To give you an example, E.W. Dijkstra, one of the pioneers of structured programming and programming methods in general, once implied that anyone who has programmed using a language that relies on the GOTO - i.e. Fortran, assembler and in particular BASIC - is beyond redemption. This is clearly ridiculous (see The myth of the evil GOTO) and doesn't even deserve an answer but it has done a lot to alienate a whole generation of microcomputer programmers.

Real languages

At the end of the day the task that falls to any programmer wanting to write well structured code is to find a way of using the facilities that each language offers to produce the standard structured elements. At its simplest you have to find a way of making conditional loops, enumeration loops, monadic (one way) selects, dyadic (two way) selects and multiple

32 The structure of control   Chapter Two

selects out of the raw materials of the language. Finding out about these basic forms is also the best way to learn a new language.

The most primitive languages currently in use, e.g. assembler, early Fortran and early BASIC expected all conditional loops to be constructed from conditional and unconditional transfer commands. For example, in Fortran a general conditional loop would be written

>   1   CONTINUE
>   *pre-exit instructions*
>   IF (*condition*) GOTO 2
>   *post-exit instructions*
>   GOTO 1
>   2   *rest of program*

where the CONTINUE statement is an unnecessary but useful marker of the start of the loop. This form of loop is easy to construct in any language that has direct transfer instructions and can be specialised to loops with exit points at the start and end and generalised to multiple exit point loops. For example, the same loop in 8088/6 assembly language would be

>   loop: *pre-exit instructions*
>   cmp   al,10h
>   jeq   lpend
>   *post-exit instructions*
>   jmp loop
>   lpend: *rest of program*

The only real difference is the way that the conditional transfer out of the loop has to be formed from a number of instructions. Most machines have a condition code register that is set according to the result of the last instruction. For example, there will generally be a zero bit or flag that is set if the result of the last operation is zero. The condition code register is used by conditional transfer instructions such as jeq label (Jump on EQual) which will transfer control to the labelled instruction only if the zero condition code bit is set. In other words 'jump if the result of the last operation was zero'. In the example the cmp al,10h compares the contents of the al register with the value 10h by subtracting one from the other hence the zero bit is set if al contains 10h.

More recent languages provide special instructions to construct conditional loops. Some take the attitude that only certain types of conditional loops are needed - i.e. WHILE, UNTIL etc. and leave you to construct any other types using the GOTO instruction. Ada and Turbo BASIC both provide a general conditional loop that doesn't involve the GOTO instruction. In Ada this is

>LOOP
>   *pre-exit instructions*
>EXIT WHEN *cond*
>   *post-exit instructions*
>END LOOP

and in Quick or Turbo BASIC

>DO
>   *pre-exit instructions*
>IF cond THEN EXIT LOOP
>   *post-exit instructions*
>LOOP

Modula-2 also provides LOOP-END and EXIT constructs.

Most other languages only provide a WHILE and an UNTIL loop. For example, in Pascal the WHILE loop is

>WHILE *cond* DO
>BEGIN
>   *list of instructions*
>END

and the UNTIL loop is

>REPEAT
>   *list of instructions*
>UNTIL *cond*

The C programming language also provides a WHILE loop as

>WHILE *(cond)*
>{
>   *list of instructions*
>}

but its UNTIL loop is written as a variant of the WHILE

>DO
>{
>   *list of instructions*
>}
>WHILE *(cond)*

When it comes to enumeration loops most languages provide explicit FOR statements that only differ in what can be enumerated. The only exception is of course assembler where an enumeration loop has to be built using an explicit counter and test. For example, in 8088/86 assembler a FOR loop could be written as

```
            mov    al,start
loop:       list of instructions
            inc    al
            cmp    al,finish
            jle    loop
```

In this example the al register is used as the loop counter which is initialised to start. The inc al instruction adds one to it each time through the loop and the cmp and jle (Jump Less or Equal) keep the loop going until al>finish. This is the exact equivalent of the more familiar BASIC FOR loop

>FOR i=start TO finish
>   *list of instructions*
>NEXT i

Real languages 35

Many machines have a special decrement and test instruction that can be used to form a more efficient FOR loop. For example the 8088/86 family has a loop *label* instruction which decrements the cx register and branches to *label* if the result isn't zero. Using this an enumeration loop can be written

```
            mov   cx,count
start:      list of instructions
            loop start
```

This repeats the body of the loop count times. Each time through the loop cx is automatically decremented until it reaches zero when the loop ends. High level languages differ very little in the facilities they provide for enumeration loops. For example, in Fortran the DO loop

```
        DO 1 i=1,10
          list of instructions
    1   CONTINUE
```

is identical to the Pascal

```
FOR i:=1 TO 10 DO
BEGIN
    list of instructions
END
```

and the BASIC

```
FOR i=1 TO 10
    list of instructions
NEXT i
```

Even the wordy Cobol

PERFORM *statement label* VARYING i FROM 1 TO 10 BY 1 UNTIL i GREATER THAN 10

is recognisable as the same construct!

Where they do differ is in flexibility. For example, in Fortran 66 the loop increment could only be one whereas in Fortran 77 it could be any integer positive or negative. In Pascal and Ada only increments of +1 or -1 are possible. For example, in Pascal

>   FOR i:=10 DOWN TO 1 DO
>   BEGIN
>   *list of instructions*
>   END

and in Ada

>   FOR i IN REVERSE 1..10 LOOP
>   list of instructions
>   END LOOP

both count down from 10 to 1. BASIC and Algol 60 go one better and allow any increment including fractional step sizes. This is really a dangerous feature because you cannot rely on the accuracy of the real arithmetic used to implement such a loop. As a result it is difficult to predict the exact set of values that the loop counter goes through, how many times the body of the loop will be executed, and the loop's exact behaviour will depend on the machine that it is run on.

Before leaving the subject of the FOR loop it is worth taking a look at the amazing FOR construct found in C. This has the general form FOR(*exp1*;*exp2*;*exp3*) where *exp1* is the initialisation expression performed once at the start of the loop, *exp2* is the test condition used for the loop to continue and *exp3* is the increment expression performed once per loop at the end of the loop. In other words

>   FOR(*exp1*;*exp2*;*exp3*)
>   {
>   *list of instructions*
>   }

is equivalent to

exp1;
while (*exp2*)
{
   list of instructions;
   exp3
}

The usual FOR loop can be written in C as {FOR i=1;i<=10;i++} where the expression i++ means increment the value of i by one. On the face of it the C FOR loop is just a confusing way of writing a simple enumeration loop but in the right hands it can be used to produce some surprising results. For example, you can enter a list of expressions each separated by commas for each of the three types of expression in a FOR statement. This can be used, for example to establish multiple loop counters as in

FOR(i=0, j=0 ;i <=100 ; i++, j=i+j)

which sets i and j to zero at the start of the loop, increments i each time through the loop and adds i to j. Every C programmer can show you a way of coding something clever using a FOR statement; sometimes they are good and sometimes bad. More often than not the C FOR statement is used to obscure meaning rather than enhance it.

Modern languages are more or less agreed on how selections should be made. Older languages, e.g. assembler, BASIC and Fortran 66, still expect the programmer to construct selections using conditional and unconditional branches. For example, in early BASIC a one way select equivalent to IF..THEN *list of statements* can be written as

10 IF NOT(cond) THEN GOTO 50
20   *list of instructions*
50 *rest of program*

Assembler uses more or less the same construct

         cmp al,const
         bne skip
             list of instructions
      skip: *rest of program*

where the condition is that the al register is equal to const.

Of course modern languages have improved on this by abandoning the use of labels and explicit transfer instructions. For example, in Pascal the same selection would be written as

> IF *cond* THEN BEGIN
> *List of instructions*
> END

Similar statements exist in later versions of BASIC, Ada, C, Fortran 77 etc..

When it comes to a two-way select then this is where modern languages make things really simple. As has already been described in older languages such as assembler, Fortran 66 and BASIC the two way select had to be written in a convoluted form. For example, in Fortran 66 the two way select would be written

> IF (*cond*) GOTO 1
>   *list of instructions*
>   . .
>   GOTO 2
> 1   *list of instructions*
>   . .
> 2   *rest of program*

The most usual mistake with this construct is to miss out the GOTO 2 instruction which of course makes the selection non-exclusive, i.e. both lists are executed if *cond* is false! Of course the familiar IF..THEN..ELSE construct is much easier and so safer to use. The only real difference between languages is the way that the end of the IF..THEN..ELSE blocks are marked. For example, in Pascal the two-way select is written

> IF *cond*   THEN BEGIN
>   *list of instructions*
>   END
> ELSE BEGIN
>   *list of instructions*
>   END

Ada, modern dialects of BASIC and Fortran 77 use END IF to terminate the IF statement as in (Modula 2 uses END)

>   IF *cond* THEN
>   *list of instructions*
>   ELSE
>   *list of instructions*
>   END IF

The greatest diversity of statements concerning selection can be seen in different language's approach to multiple selections. Complex multiple selections are generally implemented as nested IF statements. For example, (Ada, Fortran 77, BASIC, Modula 2)

>   IF *cond1* THEN
>   *list of instructions 1*
>   ELSE
>   IF *cond2* THEN
>   *list of instructions 2*
>   ELSE
>   IF *cond3* THEN
>   *list of instructions 3*
>   END IF
>   END IF
>   END IF

will select one of the three lists of instructions depending on which of *cond1*, *cond2* or *cond3* is true. If you find this difficult to see I would agree that this looks complex. To make it slightly easier Ada and Modula 2 allow it to be written as

>   IF*cond1* THEN
>   *instructions 1*
>   ELSEIF*cond2* THEN
>   *instructions 2*
>   ELSEIF *cond3* THEN
>   *instructions 3*
>   END IF
>   END IF
>   END IF

where the ELSE and the IF commands have been combined into ELSEIF. On the whole I don't think it's very much better! A particular problem in nested IFs occurs with languages that use IF statements without an explicit ENDIF due to the difficulty of deciding where one IF stops and another finishes.

For example, in the Pascal

>   IF *cond1* THEN
>   IF *cond2*   THEN BEGIN
>   *list of instructions 1*
>   END
>   ELSE BEGIN
>   *list of instructions 2*
>   END

(where the indenting has been restricted to make the ambiguity obvious) which IF statement does the ELSE belong to? Is it the first IF, in which case the second list of instructions is obeyed if *cond1* is false, or is it the second IF in which case the second list of instructions is obeyed when *cond1* is true and *cond2* is false? The answer is that in Pascal there is an extra rule which says that ELSE statements are always paired with the innermost IF, so the second interpretation is correct. Once you know this it is possible to indent the program to make this clear

>   IF *cond1* THEN
>   IF *cond2*   THEN BEGIN
>   *list of instructions 1*
>   END
>   ELSE BEGIN
>   *list of instructions 2*
>   END

Even so it is far from intuitive!

Fortunately it is not often that nested IF statements are required because the selection criterion for the set of statements is usually very simple. For example it is often the case that the value of a single expression will determine which of n statements is to be executed and this can be achieved using the CASE construct which is found in most languages.

For example in Pascal a three-way select that depends on the value in s can be written

    CASE s OF
        value1:BEGIN *list of instructions 1* END
        value2:BEGIN *list of instructions 2* END
        value3:BEGIN *list of instructions 2* END
    END

where *list of instructions 1* is obeyed if s equals *value1* and so on.. You can see that the CASE statement is equivalent to the following list of sequential IFs

    IF s=*value1* THEN BEGIN *list of instructions 1* END;
    IF s=*value2* THEN BEGIN *list of instructions 2* END;
    IF s=*value3* THEN BEGIN *list of instructions 3* END;

as long as none of the lists of instructions change the value of s. Sequential or cascaded IF statements can be used in any language that doesn't have a CASE statement.

You can see that the CASE is much simpler than the nested IF and it should be used in preference to it wherever possible.

key points

- Programs with a complex flow of control are difficult to understand, and hence to modify and debug.

- Structured programming controls the complexity of the flow of control by using only a small number of simple, and hopefully standard, control structures.

- These can be created from simpler commands, such as GOTO and IF..THEN GOTO, or can be supplied as special statements within the language.

- The standard structures are combined using sequencing and nesting.

- Jumps into or out of the standard control structures are obviously no part of a well structured program.

- Loops can be categorised according to the number of exit points and where they are placed.

- The simplest loops have one exit point.

- Real languages differ in the statements that they provide for constructing control structures but good structure is possible within even the most primitive language.

Chapter Three
Modular programming

In Chapter One it was suggested that there was a real difference between the mind of a programmer and a non-programmer. The difference was to do with the ability to think about processes and convert something which is about change into a static representation on paper. In short programmers are good at describing how to do things.

From this you might also conclude that all programmers are good at analysing how things are done, i.e. at solving new problems, but in my experience this isn't always the case. Some programmers seem to be good at it, some not so good and in any case the methods that they use vary a great deal and don't seem to be anything to do with accepted programming methods.

This makes the presentation of any theory of how new problems should be tackled particularly difficult. To a certain extent we cannot expect a full theory of how to create or invent new solutions from scratch because this would imply that we could write programs that write programs and so produce intelligent machines. All of this might be possible in the future but for the moment it takes a human mind to supply the creativity needed to solve a problem and while programmers might be better at describing solutions they are often no better than average at finding them in the first place!

Problem assembly

You might be wondering at this point how it is possible for a programmer not to be good at problem solving and yet manage to survive? Surely every program is a challenge that has to be met with the application of raw problem solving ability? Well, no. Most programmers spend their time repeating bits of program that they have used many times before. I don't mean just reinventing the wheel by rewriting programs that already exist in other languages. This certainly occupies a lot of programmer time but even when you are writing completely new programs you are drawing on your past experience. Generally you can identify all of the parts of the new program as being similar to parts of other programs that you have written in the past. This stock of program fragments is one of the main differences between a novice programmer and an old hand. After you have been programming a long time you start to think that there is nothing new and you have seen it all before. Usually this is the time that some slightly novel problem throws you off your guard and proves that you are far from knowing it all! Such problems are usually wolves in sheep's clothing. Lulled into a false sense of security you start to use your well tried methods only to discover that they don't work.

The interesting thing is that when I come across such a problem I am immediately aware that the way I am thinking is quite different. It's almost as if a different piece of the mental machinery has been turned on to tackle the task of inventing something new. This reinforces the idea that most of programming is about identifying known solutions within new problems.

In other words programming is more a question of identifying known sub-problems within an apparently new problem. Once identified the solution to these known sub-problems can be produced from stock and the only remaining difficulty is in assembling the complete solution. In other words, many programmers are good solution assemblers rather than good problem solvers.

Staying the course

An experienced programmer rarely has to solve a new problem, but how does a novice programmer become experienced without serving an apprenticeship that involves a fair amount of problem solving? If they have to solve problems from scratch to learn the required standard fragments then surely this means that only good problem solvers ever stay the course and become programmers? The answer is that novice programmers often learn the solution from other programmers, either by word of mouth or by example. Of course this isn't always the case; some novice programmers do invent all of the solutions for themselves, but this isn't a prerequisite for being becoming a successful programmer.

If you take a group of programming students at the start of a course and give them all the same set of practical exercises you will find that some solve the problems by creating the solution from almost nothing, while others somehow 'learn' of the solution. I'm not suggesting that they cheat, but one way or another they gain enough information from tutors, books or fellow students to arrive at a working program. At this stage it is tempting to think of the two groups as 'pass' and 'fail' but the amazing thing is that by the time you have reached the stage of writing BIG programs much of the difference has vanished. It seems that at the more advanced level what counts is having seen enough examples, and it doesn't matter if you invented the solution yourself or learned it from an external source! Of course the difference immediately becomes apparent again as soon as you introduce a problem that needs some new programming fragment to solve - but these are rare!

Complexity control

In most cases the production of a program is a matter of managing a large mass of detail rather than inventing anything new. Writing a small 10 or 20 line program is easy - you can keep the whole thing in your head. It also represents a single programming problem that can be solved and added to your repertoire. For example, if I were to ask you to write a program to find the total of a list of numbers you would produce something like

```
INPUT n
t=0
FOR i=1 TO n
    INPUT a
    t=t+a
NEXT i
```

If you think this is trivial then it is clearly a long time since you encountered the problem or watched a novice programmer try to solve it. The solution contains a number of general programming ideas - reading in a number to control the loop, initialising variables before a loop, running sums etc. that if you haven't seen before take a long time to invent. Once you have seen this basic building block - the **running sum** loop - it becomes part of the solution to so many other problems.

The situation is very different as soon as you consider a program with hundreds of lines. You can attempt to keep the whole thing in your head but I predict that sooner or later you will fail! I have seen very large programs written in this way, usually by self taught programmers and they are feats of mental effort. Such effort is quite unnecessary and there are easier ways of producing a better product.

Equally a large program doesn't represent a single programming problem in the same way that the 'add a list of numbers program' does. A large program will consist of many small programming challenges - most of which you will have come across before. The real problem is in putting the whole jigsaw together - or in **complexity control** as the modern jargon has it.

Most programmers, but not all, have come to realise that the best way to write a large program is to find a way of splitting it down into a collection of smaller programs or modules. Each module solves a small part of the problem and may itself use other modules in this solution. **Modular programming** is definitely a good thing. Even the first programming languages such as Fortran provided ways of creating modules or subroutines that could be used together to make larger programs. More modern languages such as Pascal and Modula 2 go to greater lengths to provide the programmer with good ways of constructing modular programs. There are even a whole class of programming languages and methods -

object oriented programming or OOPs - that concentrate almost exclusively on the modular aspects of programming.

The basic idea of a module is simply a chunk of code that can be used by another program. For example, if I put together a module called SORT that will sort a list of numbers into order, then at any point in another program I could invoke the module simply by writing its name or an instruction similar to CALL SORT. Most programmers know about modules in one form or another - the BASIC subroutine, the Fortran subroutine, the Pascal procedure, the C function and so on.. The trouble is that the quality of module that a programming language provides varies a great deal. For example, the subroutine as provided in the oldest dialects of BASIC is abysmal and is the biggest reason to criticise the language - rather than the usual crime levelled against it of promoting the use of GOTO. Modern dialects such as BBC BASIC, Turbo, Quick, Super and True BASIC have much improved subroutine facilities and they are not subject to the same failings.

A good module

The fact that some programming languages provide poor methods of constructing modules has resulted in some programmers rejecting the whole idea. This is a great pity but no doubt one day they will come across a language that does provide such facilities and then suffer a conversion.

All this raises the question of what constitutes a good module. A good module should be independent of the rest of the program in all ways apart from the few explicit ways provided for it to interact with other modules. The old fashioned BASIC subroutine is an ideal example of how not to create a module. All that was provided was a GOSUB x command which transferred control to line number x and a RETURN command which transferred control back to the line following the GOSUB. You could use GOSUB and RETURN to create a module but this was not isolated from the rest of the program. In particular the programmer had to be careful to use different variables within the subroutine to avoid accidentally changing variables in the main program. For example, if you created a module that printed ten blank lines

```
1000 FOR i=1 TO 10
1010    PRINT
1020 NEXT i
1030 RETURN
```

you could use it from any point in your program simply by typing GOSUB 1000. But watch out if your main program is using i for some other purpose! In this case i is a **global variable** and it is shared by all subroutines that make up the program. Such accidental changing of the value in a variable by a subroutine is usually referred to as a **side effect**. Even if you manage to cope with using variables that are common to all subroutines in a program there is no easy way of creating subroutine libraries because of the problem of allocating line numbers.

To find a reasonable method of constructing modules you have to look to Turbo/Quick or BBC BASIC or languages such as Fortran, Pascal etc.. For example, in Turbo/Quick BASIC you can construct a 'ten blank line' subroutine using SUB and END SUB -

```
SUB blank
FOR i=1 TO 10
    PRINT
NEXT i
END SUB
```

This subroutine can be used by writing CALL blank anywhere that it is needed. In this case the variable i has nothing to do with any variable called i in any other part of the program or other subroutines. In other words i is local to the subroutine - it is a **local variable**.

Clearly subroutine blank cannot produce any side effects. The advantage of this is that you can concentrate on writing subroutine blank without having to worry about the details of any other part of the program. This alone makes it possible to write a large program by breaking it down into a collection of smaller programs.

```
    SUB blank
    FOR i=1 TO 10
    PRINT
    NEXT i
    END SUB
```

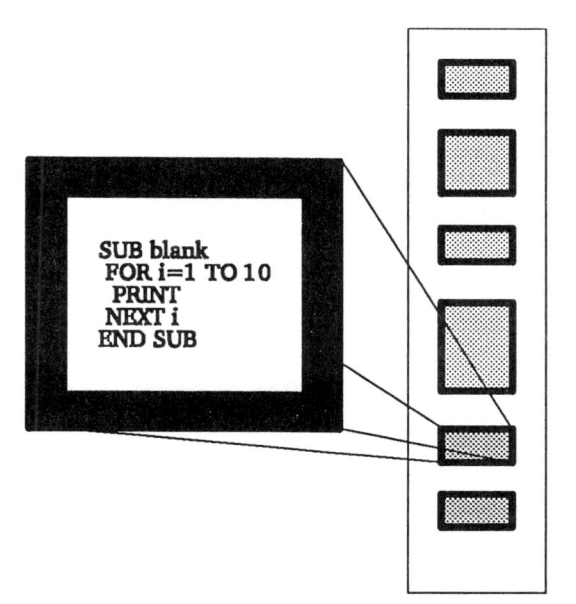

A subroutine should be isolated from the rest of the program

If you hope to write a large program as a collection of smaller subprograms then it is clear that you have to insist that all of the subprogram's variables are local. Some languages make this the default, others use more complex rules that define whether a variable is accessible or not - see Chapter Four.

Desirable interactions

So much for controlling unwanted interactions but what about making subroutines work together. You cannot build a large program out of a collection of smaller programs if the said smaller programs are all entirely independent of one another! There has to be some way for information to get into a module and some way for it to get out. Most programmers have come across the idea of a **parameter** before as a way of passing data into and out of a subroutine but even if you are familiar with it the idea can be very subtle.

A parameter is a special variable that can be used to transfer data into or out of a module. For example, in the following version of subroutine blank

> SUB blank(n)
> FOR i=1 TO n
>   PRINT
> NEXT i
> END SUB

n is called a **formal parameter**. It has nothing to do with any other variable called n in any other program or subroutine. To pass a value to n within the subroutine you would simply call it using something like CALL blank(10). In this case 10 is called an **actual parameter**. This assigns the value 10 to n and then starts the subroutine going. This is easy to understand. Many beginners find calls such as CALL blank(a) more difficult to understand but the mechanism is just the same. The value in a, the actual parameter, is transferred to n, the formal parameter and the subroutine is started. The real test of confidence is what does CALL blank(n) do? Exactly the same. The fact that the name of the variable in the call and the parameter are the same is only confusing to humans.

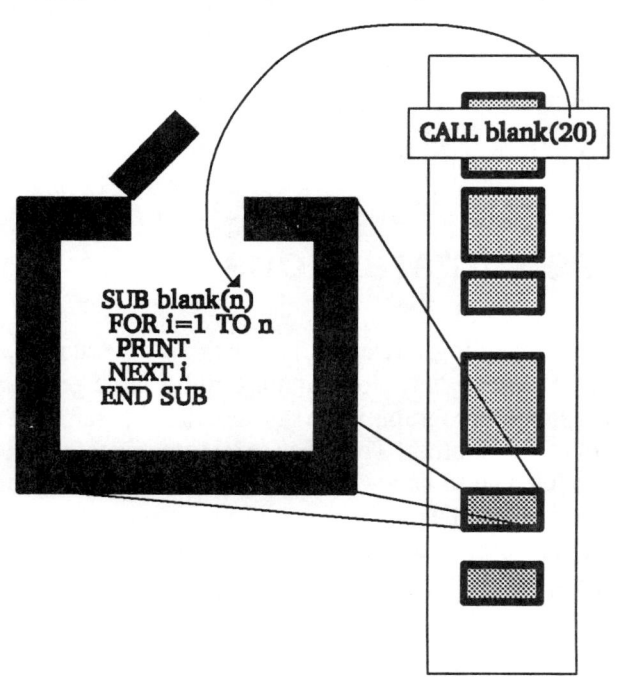

An input parameter provides a way for data to get into a subroutine

You can think of the call command as making a temporary connection between the variable used as the actual parameter and the formal parameter in the subroutine. In the case of Turbo/Quick BASIC any changes made to n in subroutine blank are also passed back to the variable used in the call. For example, if the line n=100 is added to the end of blank then, after CALL blank(a), the variable a would contain 100. In other words the connection is two way and the parameter does affect the variable used in the call.

Sometimes it is desirable to restrict the way a parameter works so that it cannot affect the variable in the calling program. Such a parameter can only be used to pass data into a subroutine. In Turbo/Quick BASIC for example, you can stop a parameter passing data back from the subroutine by calling it using an expression. For example, in CALL blank(10) there is no way that changing n can change the value of the constant 10. The same is true for CALL blank(2*a+10). That is, n does not affect any part of the expression 2*a+10. The subtle point is that in Turbo/Quick BASIC there is a world of difference between CALL blank(a) and CALL blank(+a). The first allows the subroutine to change the value of a, the second disallows it. In languages such as Pascal this difference is made more clear by the use of a keyword to define the type of a parameter. For example, in Pascal the procedure

```
PROCEDURE blank(n:INTEGER);
VAR i:INTEGER;
 FOR i:=1 TO n DO WRITELN;
 n:=100;
END
```

would have no effect on the variable used to call it, but the procedure

```
PROCEDURE blank(VAR n:INTEGER);
VAR i:INTEGER;
 FOR i:=1 TO n DO WRITELN;
 n:=100;
END
```

would. That is, in Pascal a parameter carries data into but not out of a procedure unless the word VAR is used in the procedure definition to make a two-way connection.

52 Modular programming — Chapter Three

In general you can see that parameters are going to be one of three possible types

1) **input parameters** that pass data into, but not out of, a module
2) **output parameters** that pass data out of, but not into, a module
and
3) **input/output parameters** that pass data into and out of a module.

Older languages often don't make adequate distinctions between these types of parameter but newer languages such as Ada go to a lot of trouble to make it absolutely clear what is going on. In Ada you can define a parameter as being 'in', 'out' or 'input'. For example, in the Ada procedure

```
PROCEDURE add(n:IN integer;t:OUT integer) IS
  a:integer;
BEGIN
  t:=0;
  FOR i IN 1..n LOOP
    GET(a);
    t:=t+a;
  END LOOP;
END add;
```

the variable n is an input parameter and can only pass data into the procedure. Any changes to n within add do not affect any variable in any other part of the program. However variable t is an output parameter and carries no data into the procedure.

Even if the language that you are using doesn't provide any facilities for distinguishing between input, output and input/output parameters you should still think in these terms, and even invent your own conventions to make clear what is happening. For example, in BASIC you could add comments to the start of every subroutine listing the parameters and whether they are used for input, output or input/output.

How to pass parameters?

Once you understand that parameters are a way of controlling the interaction between subroutines then their desirable properties become obvious. Unfortunately there are a variety of ways that parameter passing can be implemented and these have slightly different properties.

The parameter passing mechanism described earlier where the contents of the actual parameter are transferred to the formal parameter is known as **call by value**. Call by value can be used to implement both input, output and input/output parameters. If a parameter is an input-only parameter then the value of the actual parameter is transferred to the formal parameter at the start of the routine. If the parameter is an output-only parameter then the value of the formal parameter is transferred to the actual parameter at the end of the routine.

Call by value satisfies most requirements except storage efficiency. Having a copy of an actual parameter within a subroutine makes very little difference unless the parameter is something more than a simple variable - an array say. In this case the memory and time required to make a complete copy of the formal parameter may be prohibitive. The most common solution to this problem is to use **call by reference**. In this case the parameter in the subroutine is used as a pointer to the actual parameter. This means that all operations on the parameter in the subroutine really do make use of the actual parameter in the calling routine. You can see that, unless restricted in some way, call by reference produces an input/output parameter. To produce an input-only parameter you need to add the rule that any changes to the parameter within the subroutine, i.e. assignments, are illegal. This makes the parameter behave like a named constant rather than a variable. Call by reference is used by most modern languages and because of it there is never any need to claim that considerations of efficiency mean that you cannot use parameters to pass data into or out of a subroutine.

There are a number of other parameter passing mechanisms but they are all variations on call by value or call by reference. Apart from considerations of efficiency, the only real differences occur when the same actual parameter is passed to two different formal parameters. This results in a single variable in the calling program being referred to by two different names in the subroutine hence the name **aliasing**.

Aliasing can arise in two different ways, either because a global variable is passed to a subroutine or because the same variable is passed more than once. For example, if the array t is a global variable then, ignoring other side effects, the subroutine

```
SUB swap(x,y)
t=y
y=x
x=t
END SUB
```

will work. However if you try to work out what happens in the call

```
CALL swap(t,a)
```

then you might begin to see the difficulties.

If call by value is being used then the swap will work because the value of t is transferred into x and a into y at the time of the call. If call by reference is being used then the results are very different. In this case x is set to point at variable t in the main program which is of course the same as the t variable in the subroutine. With this in mind a better reflection of what the program does is

```
t=a
a=t
t=t
```

which is not a swap of t and a. This behaviour depends on t being global and it should be regarded as highly abnormal programming. Its sole purpose is to illustrate the difference between call by value and reference.

A more likely source of aliasing is the use of the same actual parameter more than once. In the case of the swap subroutine, with t a local variable this time, this corresponds to the call

```
CALL swap(a,a)
```

which of course results in a being swapped with itself. In this case the behaviour is reasonable, but consider the aliasing produced in using the subroutine

```
SUB max(x,y,z)
z=y
IF x>y THEN z=x
END SUB
```

with the call CALL max(a,b,a) which clearly is intended to find the larger of a and b and store it in a. If call by value is used then everything works as expected because z is a variable distinct from x. However if call by reference is used then x and z are aliases for a and the subroutine performs an operation best summed up by

```
a=y
IF a>y THEN a=y
```

In other words the subroutine simply stores y in a, no matter what the initial value of a is.

It is important to be aware of the danger of aliasing. It is always easy to avoid the aliasing that is produced by global variables and parameters referring to one another, but the temptation to use the same actual parameter more than once in a subroutine call often seems a safe and natural thing to do. Some languages actually try to make such parameter aliasing illegal. This is easy enough to enforce in examples such as CALL swap(a,a) but what about CALL swap(a(i),a(j)) this only becomes illegal if and when i = j. Such cases can make it very difficult to spot an aliasing error.

One interesting variant of parameter passing that can be found in Ada is **named association**. Normally actual and formal parameters are matched up on the basis of their position but there is no reason why other methods cannot be used. In named association the name of the formal parameter is quoted in the call and the position of the actual parameters is irrelevant.

For example, the Ada procedure

PROCEDURE max(a,b :IN integer; ans:OUT integer) IS *etc.*

could be called as max(1,2,x) in the usual way with the parameters matching up by position. However if the call is max(ans=>x,b<=2,a<=1) then the parameters are assigned exactly the same values as in the first call even though their positions are very different.

The C trap

C is particularly primitive in its parameter passing methods. All parameters are passed as input-only parameters and to simulate an output or an input/output parameter you have to pass its address. Once the procedure has the address of a parameter it can modify it more or less directly. You should be able to see that this is a sort of manual pass by reference. This approach to parameter passing has big problems in that how a parameter is passed can depend on where it is passed from. For example, the function add(n,t) would have to be called as add(m,&total) so that the value of m was passed in to n and the address of total was passed into to t. However, suppose that add is being used from within another function and total was itself passed in as an address. In this case add is being passed the address of an address which wasn't the programmer's intention at all. The correct form of the call would be add(m,total). This strange parameter passing is one of the main reasons that C is half way between a high level and a low level language. The problem has been put right in C++ with the introduction of an automatic pass by reference.

How many and what type?

In many languages parameter passing is very crude. Even fairly modern languages such as Pascal only go so far. For example, there are plenty of situations in which it would be an advantage for the number of parameters to vary. For example, the best known is Pascal's built in READ and WRITE procedures which will accept a list of parameters to be read or written as in READ(a,b,c) and WRITE(a,b,c,d,e). Assembly language programmers have been using subroutines with variable numbers of parameters for a long time. They are generally implemented by pushing the parameters on the system stack (see Chapter Five) and then pushing as the last item the number of parameters that the subroutine should recover. However it seems to have proved to be difficult to implement the same feature in a high level language. For example, Pascal allows the supplied procedures READ and WRITE to have a variable number of parameters but no other procedures can follow their lead. In other words, Pascal makes an exception for its own convenience.

The only conventional programming language that I know of that provides something close to a variable parameter facility is Ada. In an Ada procedure you can define a default value for any IN parameters. This default is used to initialise the parameter if it is left out of a call. This is clearly more limited than allowing any number of parameters but it is a step in the right direction. Some older languages allow a variable number of parameters by accident because they don't bother to check that the number of parameters in a function call corresponds to the number of parameters in the definition! Depending on the actual method used to pass the parameters, such a mismatch could sometimes be used without crashing the program. Obviously such out of the ordinary use of a language isn't reliable and should be avoided at all costs!

If a language performs type checking, i.e. ensuring that data is always of the same type as the variable that it is being stored in (see Chapter Five), then the issue of parameter type also arises. If you are supposed to pass a character variable then a character variable is what most languages will insist you pass. However in the real world you very often need a subroutine that performs more or less the same actions on different types of data. For example, the subroutine

```
SUB max(a,b,ans)
IF a>b THEN
    ans=a
ELSE
    ans=b
END IF
```

is a recipe for finding the maximum of two numbers irrespective of their type, integer, real or complex but many languages will insist that it works only on numbers that correspond to the type of its parameters. Hence in Fortran you have to have a function defined for each numeric type - IMAX for integers, RMAX for reals, CMAX for complex etc..

A better approach is **operator overloading** where there can be more than one subroutine with the same name and the correct one is selected depending on the types of parameter used in the call. For example, in Ada if you define the two procedures

PROCEDURE max(a,b:IN integer;ans:OUT integer) IS *etc.*

PROCEDURE max(a,b:IN real;ans:OUT real) IS *etc.*

where of course you also fill in the body of the procedure more or less identically, then the call max(6.1,8.9,ans) would call the second procedure and max(1,2,ians) would call the first version of the procedure. You can see that operator overloading allows a uniformity of treatment that appears simple to use, even if it is a lot of extra work to create!

Unfortunately operator overloading isn't particularly widespread in current languages. Most object oriented languages offer it, C++ for example, but apart from that category only Ada supports it. This causes a problem for languages that provide I/O procedures. For example, Pascal's READ and WRITE procedures not only break the rules by allowing a variable number of parameters, they also allow the parameters to be of different type. Modula-2 doesn't have operator overloading but still provides its I/O facilities by way of procedures. As it plays fair by its own rules this means that it has to supply an I/O function for each data type, for example, WRITEINT, WRITEREAL etc.. This is very irritating and shows just how much a mechanism like operator overloading is needed in a modern language.

Ada also supports the use of **generic units**. A generic unit is a procedure specification which acts as a template for an actual procedure. You can use parameters in the specification to modify details that would normally be fixed in a normal procedure definition. For example, you could use a parameter to specify the type of the variables to be used by the procedure and then create as many version of the procedure as were necessary to deal with different data types. A generic unit is very similar to the concept of a macro processor, where parameters are used to specify items of text to be changed to produce the desired text.

Functions and expressions

In the same way that a large program can be made up of subroutines, an **operator expression** can be made up of functions. Operator expressions - arithmetic expressions, logical expressions, character expressions etc.- haven't been mentioned until this point mostly because they are well known by every programmer. An operator expression gives the programmer the ability to combine any number of data values of a given type and produce a single new value of the same type. For example

$$a=b*12-c$$

is an arithmetic expression that combines the simple values stored in b and c and the constant 12, produces a single result and stores it in a. Notice that implicit in the use of an expression is the idea that the single result produced can be stored or assigned in a variable. If more than one result of the type were produced the concept of assignment would be impossible to use. However it is important to notice that this restriction is to a single result of the given type not a single value. For example, there is no reason why the expression

$$a=b*c$$

should not be applied to arrays with the appropriate definition of * to mean matrix multiplication say. In this case the result is a single array of data which can be assigned to the array a. In practice such advanced expressions are often beyond the power of modern languages. (However it is worth commenting that APL is virtually based on the use of this idea!)

A function is best thought of as a special sort of subroutine that returns a single value in such a way that it can be incorporated into an expression. For example, the procedure max that finds the maximum of two numbers given earlier is best written as a function. In Fortran this function would be written

```
FUNCTION max(i , j)
max=j
IF (i.GT.j) max=i
RETURN
```

Notice that the function's name, max, is used as if it was a variable. When the function ends the single value that it returns is the final value stored in max. This use of the function's name to return results is quite common although many languages avoid it because it isn't as clear as using an explicit instruction that determines the return value. For example, in Modula 2 the max function would be written

```
PROCEDURE max(i,j:integer):integer
BEGIN
IF i>j THEN
    RETURN (i)
ELSE
    RETURN (j)
END IF
END max
```

In this case the value of the function is determined by which RETURN (value) instruction is obeyed. Notice however that the association between the function name and value isn't completely broken because max is defined to be integer by the first line!

Once a function is defined it can be used within expressions just as if it was a variable of the appropriate type. For example

a=b+max(c,d)

assigns the sum of b and the maximum of c and d to a.

Once you realise that functions are used in this way it becomes clear that they shouldn't return more than one value. Indeed they should not affect the program in any other way. In other words, they should have no side effects. For example, suppose you include the command PRINT "Hello" in the max function, which is perfectly legal in most languages, then using max in an expression would alter the screen display! A function that does anything that could be categorised as unexpected is a bad function.

Functions are the building blocks of complex expressions but occasionally their use is cumbersome. It has occurred to many a programmer that it would be nice to use functions as if they were new operators rather than variables. For example, instead of the max(a,b) function one could define the a!b operator to mean the largest of a or b. Once defined you could then write expressions such as a=b+c!d instead of a=b+max(c,d). This simple idea turns out to be very difficult to implement because of the complications introduced by the way operators interact. For example, what does c!d+e mean? Is it (c!d)+e or is it c!(d+e)? The answer depends on the way the relative priorities are assigned to ! and +.

Because of these difficulties very few languages allow you to define new operators, Prolog being the notable exception. However some languages allow you to redefine or extend existing operators. For example, Ada will allow you to name a function +, -, * or / and the function will be used in place of the usual + operator when the parameter types match those of the new function - i.e. operator overloading is used to decide when your new operator is appropriate.

Cohesion and coupling

Parameters are clearly important in building large programs from smaller units. They control the flow of data through the program in a way that is visible and easy to understand. However in practice the story is often a little different. For example, consider the task of writing a large program that uses a number of arrays. These arrays are defined early in the program and used by almost every other part of the program. As a consequence every subroutine call has to include each of the arrays as parameters. When added to the usual odds and ends that have to be passed to each subroutine a typical call might look something like

CALL exp(mean, total, data1,output2,count,error,sum,xdata,ydata)

or even worse! Many programmers object to having to type such long parameter lists. Indeed there is a case for saying that long parameter lists of this sort are too difficult to understand and so obscure the purpose of the subroutine.

Oddly this is not a problem that has received very much attention and there are no generally accepted solutions or even points of view. Obviously subroutines should be created so that the information to be passed between them is of a reasonable volume, but how can this be achieved?

You might say that the mark of a good subroutine is that its interface with the outside world is reasonable but this still doesn't help with finding such subroutines.

You can call on ideas such as **cohesion** and **coupling** to describe this desirable property in other ways. Cohesion is the degree to which a subroutine is concerned with a single task. Of course this begs the question of what constitutes a single task and various vague and complex definitions have been proposed. When you examine them carefully all definitions of cohesion reduce to a series of examples. Even so it is common sense that a good subroutine has a high degree of cohesion. Coupling, on the other hand, measures the degree of interaction between subroutines. Clearly if two subroutines are highly coupled they have to pass large quantities of data between each other. If two subroutines are that highly coupled then it would make sense to combine them into a single unit. Hence it is usually said that a good subroutine has high cohesion and low coupling - but this still leaves us with the problem of creating such things! One solution is the object oriented approach which tends to produce highly cohesive objects with a low coupling. However this topic is best described after we have taken a look at the whole topic of data and its role in programming.

Global data

One possible solution to the problem of large parameter lists is to take all of the common data items out of the parameter list and create them as global variables accessible to all of the subroutines. One problem with this method has already been described in the section on aliasing. If a data item is passed to a subroutine, as well as being accessible because it is global, then the subroutine may not work as expected. Even if this objection is removed, having a subroutine work on a global data item reduces its potential for reuse. For example, which would you rather have a subroutine sort(x,n) which will sort the array passed as x of length n into order or a subroutine sort(n) which will sort the global variable x of length n into order. It is true that sort(n) has a smaller parameter list but it will only sort an array called x into order whereas the second version can be used to sort any array into order.

In practice it can sometimes be a simplification to make any central data structures such as arrays or records (see Chapter Five) global. As long as these are clearly described at the start of the program, and all of the subroutines work on these central data items, then this reduces the scope for confusion.

Many languages provide more subtle mechanisms for sharing data as global data. For example, Pascal uses an automatically hierarchical data sharing method which does have some advantages (see Chapter Four). Global variables are even available in older languages such as Fortran's COMMON statement. Any variables named in a COMMON statement are accessible to any subroutine containing the same COMMON statement. As COMMON areas can be named this means that different groups of subroutines can share data in a very complex way. In addition, as variables are matched up on a positional basis, shared variables can even be called by different names.

For example, in the three subroutines

```
SUBROUTINE one
COMMON /A/ a,b,c
COMMON /B/ d,e,f
RETURN

SUBROUTINE two
COMMON /A/ a,b,c
RETURN

SUBROUTINE three
COMMON /A/ a,b,c
COMMON /B/ x,y,z
RETURN
```

because of the way the COMMON statements are included, subroutine one's a,b and c are the same as a,b and c in subroutines two and three. However subroutine one's d,e and f are not accessible in subroutine two and even though they are accessible in subroutine three they are called x,y and z. Confused? Well so were a lot of Fortran programmers!

In the main Fortran's COMMON was used as a way of conserving storage space and avoiding parameters. Of course, as a COMMON statement had to be included in every subroutine that needed access to the variables, nothing was gained because the COMMON was as long as the parameter list it replaced! Surprisingly the COMMON statement can be used to implement one of the newest ideas in programming - information hiding.

Larger modules - information hiding

Although global data can sometimes be useful, the modern trend of information hiding is moving in entirely the opposite direction. Consider a group of subroutines all of which work with the same array. One subroutine may sort it, another may print it, and yet another may input data to it. If you follow the ideas of the previous section then presumably you have a choice of passing the array as a parameter or making it global to the suit of subroutines. In either case the array will be accessible to the rest, or at least a large part, of the program. Suppose that sorting, output and input are the only operations that you are prepared to allow then having it visible in this way makes it tempting for other programmers (including yourself) to use it in ways that you never intended.

This may not appear harmful but in using the array directly they are making use of the details of implementation of the subroutines rather than just a knowledge of what the subroutines do. To see that this might be harmful just consider what would happen if you decided to change the implementation from using an array to using a disk file. Following this all of the direct accesses to the array would be invalid but those that used the subroutines that you provided would still be fine.

The idea of keeping the details of implementation hidden is known as **information hiding**. In this case you can see that once again the only way that subroutines can be allowed to interact is via their parameters. In addition though there is the assumption that a subroutine will be provided for every mode of access and operation that will be required and all others are considered illegal.

Thus information hiding implies the existence of a suit of subroutines that all work together on the same data. A number of languages, Modula-2, Ada for example provide ways of grouping together subroutines with the intent of information hiding. In Ada such a grouping is called a **package** and in Modula-2 it is called a **module**.

An Ada package consists of two parts - a **package specification** and a **package body**. The package specification defines all of the externally visible details of a package. It is concerned with what the package does. The package body is a collection of functions and procedures that implement what the package is supposed to do. It is concerned with the 'how' of what the package does. Only variables declared in the package specification are accessible from outside the package. A program that wants to make use of the package has to include a context clause that **imports** all of the potentially visible items in the package specification.

Modula-2 uses the same scheme of a definition part, called the definition module and an implementation part, called the implementation module, but with the difference that data items that are visible from the outside world have to be explicitly named in an **export** statement. As it is usual for all of the variables in the definition module to be exported, the export statement represents no advance over the Ada method of exporting everything by default. A program that wants to use the variables offered for export must include an import statement that lists each variable to be imported. This is sometimes more useful than Ada's approach of importing either nothing or everything a package has to offer.

One surprising twist of fate is the fact that the old Fortran COMMON statement is ideal for implementing information hiding. If a subroutine needs to make use of data so that it is shared with other subroutines but hidden from the outside world, then a named common area can be established using

COMMON /*name* / *list of data items*

This statement can be included in any subroutine that needs to share this data and left out of the remainder. The common area can then only be accessed by other parts of the program by calling the subroutines provided for the job. In this case the definition part of the suit of subroutines is simply their names and calling conventions and they themselves form the implementation part. Which perhaps goes to show that it is difficult to invent anything completely new in computing.

Information hiding also has a connection with the object oriented approach to programming. In fact you could say that a package or module is a primitive sort of data object that is characterised more by what it does than how it does it. This topic is taken up again in Chapters Six and Seven.

Existence

Although you will find much discussion of local and global variables the related topic of when a variable exists or not is often ignored. Local and global are terms that describe a variable's accessibility or visibility from various parts of the program. More generally this is known as the **scope** of a variable.

As well as the visibility of a variable there is also the question of when it is brought into existence and when it is removed. This is sometimes referred to as the **extent** of a variable. The simplest scheme is to bring all of the variables used by the program into existence when the program starts and dispose of them when it ends. This is referred to as a **static allocation** scheme. The alternative is to create the variables that a subroutine uses when it is being used and dispose of them when it comes to an end. This is known as **dynamic allocation** and it has become the norm for most modern languages. I say the norm, but the sad fact is that many languages don't consider it part of the language definition to say when variables exist. For example, most Fortran implementations use static allocation but this is just tradition because there is nothing in the definition of Fortran that says that this is how it should be done.

The rationale for variables only existing when their subroutine is being executed is easy to appreciate. If a variable is local to a subroutine it is only visible from that subroutine, and hence can only be used from within it. From this point of view an inaccessible variable might as well not exist when its subroutine is inactive but this isn't the whole story. Consider the following BASIC subroutine

```
SUB count
i=i+1
PRINT i
END SUB
```

This is bad style because the initial value of i isn't explicitly stated, but BASIC initialises variables to zero when they are created. The intention of this subroutine is to count the number of times that it is used. Of course this depends on i being a static variable. If it is a dynamic variable then it is recreated each time the subroutine is called and so the counter never gets beyond one! In Turbo/Quick BASIC variables are static and local by default but they can be made dynamic by using the command LOCAL i and explicitly declared as static using the command STATIC i. Notice that if a variable is global then for obvious reasons it has to be static. C also allows the use of STATIC to signify that a local variable is to be kept between calls. The only way that this can be achieved in Pascal is to make the variable global, so extending its scope to extend its existence. This approach helps propagate the confusion between scope and existence.

If you think this example is not worth the fuss then consider the effect of dynamic storage allocation on information hiding in packages and modules as described earlier. If the data structures are recreated each time the package or module is entered, then there is no way that they can provide a service to the rest of the program over a period of time and the only alternative is to go back to making the data structures global and so visible from the rest of the program. Ada solves this problem by making all variables declared in the package body static. In Modula-2 all of the variables declared in a module remain in existence while any outer module is active. This means that static local variables can be created by a suitable nesting of module definitions.

For such an important characteristic language designers, manual and textbook writers are surprisingly reticent on the subject of when a variable exists and when it doesn't.

key points

- Programmers have to be good solution assemblers but they are not necessarily good problem solvers and the difference between an experienced and a novice programmer is the number of stock solutions they can draw on.

- A large program is best assembled from smaller units called subroutines or procedures. Operator expressions can be assembled from functions which return only a single value.

- The interaction between subroutines has to be controlled to avoid accidental side effects by using local variables and parameters.

- In practice parameters are implemented in a variety of ways each of which has its own advantages and disadvantages.

- A good subroutine shows a high degree of cohesion and low coupling.

- Subroutines can often be organised into larger groupings called modules or packages and control access to common data using information hiding. The existence rule for local data then becomes important.

Chapter Four
The hierarchy

It is not difficult to see that we should use subroutines or modules to build our programs, but this leaves open the question of exactly how we should use them. We can create modules that perform small tasks which are then used to piece together a larger program. As long as the modules have the desirable properties of keeping themselves to themselves and interacting with each other only in ways that the programmer specifies, the problem of fitting them together is simple. All this means that no modern programmer would ever dream of writing a large program as one undigestible chunk but would choose to put it together from bite size pieces.

The program pyramid

This is a nice theory but it ignores the important fact that in practice problems are presented to programmers in single, totally undigestible, chunks that have to be broken down in to mind sized sub-problems. In other words part of the skill of programming is dividing up a problem so that it can be solved easily and clearly. Surprisingly it turns out that irrespective of the method that you use to achieve this, the overall structure of the resulting program follows a hierarchy of modules.

It isn't difficult to see why this is true. If you are faced with a big and complex problem then you are likely to be able to see it as being composed of a number of stages. For example, many problems fall into the pattern

- get some input, work out some results and print the results. Clearly this can be implemented as a three module program

```
CALL getdata
CALL workout
CALL printresult
```

Of course in most real problems each of the three modules would still represent the solution to a fairly large problem. If you follow the religion of modular programming then your instinctive reaction will be to consider each of the subroutines as a completely new problem and proceed to divide each of them up still further. For example, you might decide that getdata is composed of two modules

```
SUB getdata
DO
     CALL message
     CALL getvalue
LOOP UNTIL fin=true
END SUB
```

which are of course smaller still. This sub-division of each of the modules would continue until the size of the resulting module was sufficiently small to be immediately comprehensible to even the dimmest programmer. At this point the sub-division stops.

From this description you can see that a modular program is inherently **hierarchical** - the main program calls a first 'layer' of modules, which in turn call a second layer and so on. Each layer uses the modules in the layer below to complete its task. You can draw a diagram, the **structure diagram,** to show this hierarchical relationship.

For example,

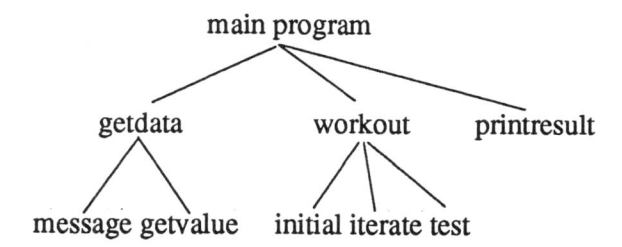

```
                    main program
                   /     |      \
            getdata    workout   printresult
            /   \      / | \
    message  getvalue initial iterate test
```

A real program would have many more modules and levels but the idea is the same. Although you may have seen this sort of diagram many times you may not have got the all of the goodness out of it! If you assume that the modules at each level are written from left to right in the order that they are called then you can get the feel for what the program does by reading across each level. For example, at the first level the program is getdata, workout and printresult, at the second it is message, getvalue, initial, iterate, test and printresult. Moving up and down the hierarchy in this way corresponds to taking coarser and finer views of the program. It is almost like altering the magnification on a microscope. At low power (top levels) all you see is the large scale features. At higher power you can see all of the details of the smallest modules that make up the program but lose sight of the whole picture.

The modules in the first level will generally require a different number of stages of splitting to complete. For example, getdata and workout need another level of modules to implement, but printdata is complete at level one. You should be able to see that the number of levels of modules needed to implement any given module is a good indication of how complex it is. Simple modules are completed in a few sub-divisions, but more complex modules need a great many levels of sub-division to produce a module that is simple enough to write.

The great idea

The fact that the natural modular structure for a program is a hierarchy has influenced many programming ideas - from suggestions about how we go about creating programs to the way Pascal treats local variables. The trouble is that much of the argument is often expressed the other way around. The common explanation is that programs have a hierarchical structure because of the application of these ideas.

In truth these ideas are only relevant because programs have a hierarchical structure more or less independently of what you choose to do about it. It is more a question of whether you acknowledge the fact and make use of it or stubbornly attempt to ignore it.

Stepwise refinement

Many programmers first meet the idea of a hierarchy of modules by way of the programming method called **stepwise refinement**. This turns the hierarchy into a method of solving problems. All you have to do, or so the method goes, is to write down the names of the first level of modules and at least you have made a start.

Put like this stepwise refinement seems a bit pointless because writing down the names of the first level of modules is either a very slight achievement or reflects the fact that you have a deep understanding of the total solution depending on how you look at it. For example, if you want to write a program to play chess then stepwise refinement says that you should begin by writing

```
CALL setup
CALL playgame
CALL result
END
```

If you include dummy subroutines or **stubs** such as

>   SUB setup
>   PRINT "setup called"
>   END SUB

you can even run and begin to test the program. In other words using stepwise refinement you can also use **stepwise testing**. You can then go on to solve the problem by expanding the definitions of setup, playgame and result. In this way the program to play chess is indeed built up in a stepwise fashion - or is it?

The question really is what is in the programmer's mind when the first level of modules is written? It could be that the programmer has a pretty good idea of how to write a chess playing program and the stepwise refinement is just a way of controlling its complexity. Or it could be that the programmer has no idea how to write a chess program and stepwise refinement is just a way of putting off the evil day when the truth has to be faced - i.e. when the playgame module is further expanded!

Although stepwise refinement is often taught as a problem solving method it really seems to be at its best as a method of organising, implementing or describing a known solution. This is a little unfair to the method because it can sometimes allow a programmer to identify and isolate the really difficult parts of a problem in the way that the playgame module encapsulates the difficult bit of the chess playing program.

If you are an experienced programmer, perhaps brought up on the stepwise refinement method, then you might find my objections to it very objectionable! I have to admit that when I sit down to write a program I naturally organise my attempts using stepwise refinement and it usually goes so much the better for it. However this just bears out the criticism of the method. I usually know or at least have a very good idea of what the program is going to do and I use stepwise refinement as a framework that I hang my ideas on.

If you have ever watched a complete beginner working on a problem that they have never solved, and never even seen the solution to, you will quickly realise that stepwise refinement only helps them organise the parts of the solution that they do already know! I am afraid that the success of stepwise refinement as a program creation method is more to do with the observation, introduced in Chapter Three, that most of the time programmers are not solving completely new problems but just rearranging fragments of known solutions to produce the desired program behaviour. We still do not know how we solve completely new programming problems because we don't know how we solve problems in general.

Don't be put off by this negative conclusion. Modular programming using stepwise refinement is still an excellent tool in our fight against the overwhelming complexity of large programs, even if it isn't very much help in creating new ideas.

Top down or bottom up

Given that the hierarchy is a good description of the program that you are trying to write, there are two possible ways of tackling the task - from the **top down,** as described by stepwise refinement or **bottom up.** A bottom up approach would be to write the most basic subroutines in the hierarchy first and then use them to make more sophisticated subroutines. The pure bottom up approach is generally not to be recommended because it is difficult to anticipate what low level subroutines will be needed for any particular program. However it is not entirely a lost cause as the existence of many subroutine libraries testifies. It can often be a useful first step to produce a library of basic functions and procedures before embarking on a major project.

In practice programmers tend to fill in the structure of a program in a number of passes, so making the entire process neither top down nor bottom up. The reasons for completing any particular part of the hierarchy first vary considerably, but a common approach is to want to tackle the difficult bits first. This usually isn't possible without having to complete, at least partially, the routines that the difficult bits depend on. For example, a programmer will often complete the I/O modules just enough to see some results and then work on the inner and more interesting part of a program. Once this is complete attention will be returned to polishing the I/O modules etc..

This repeated refinement and modification of routines in the strict order of the levels in the hierarchy is one reason why many experienced programmers have rejected stepwise refinement as being unrealistic. In a sense they are correct because stepwise refinement is an ideal description of your program at any particular stage in its development, but it isn't necessarily an accurate representation of the order that you tackled the modules in. It represents the skeleton of the program on which it is the programmer's responsibility to hang the flesh.

There is another difficulty in the hierarchical description of a program that is usually glossed over - **module reuse**. In the bottom up approach it is usually assumed that the basic routines created will be general enough to be used more than once. This corresponds to the modern notion of reusable **software components**. On the other hand, the top down approach assumes that each routine is specially created to solve a particular problem and so any reuse is fortuitous, or perhaps a nuisance. For example, there is the problem of how to show reuse in a structure diagram. Should the reused module be shown once with multiple lines leading to it from each higher level module that uses it, or should it be shown each time it is used? The multiple lines approach makes the hierarchy difficult to see and draw and in this sense drawing multiple copies of the module is easier.

At a more naive level of programming it is often suggested that a good reason for using subroutines to construct a program is that you might save yourself repeating the same lines of code by reusing it. This is true but, as this and the previous chapter have attempted to demonstrate it isn't the best reason for using subroutines. In the opinion of some programmers, software reuse of this sort is even slightly suspect. The reason is that if a low level routine is used by more than one higher level module they may require different services from it. This might be fine in the current version of the routine but come the day that the low level routine is modified this might cease to be true. The programmer doing the modification might not notice all of the uses of the low level routine and might modify it to suit only the visible ones. The solution to this problem is to include an accurate definition of what the low level routine has to do in the routine itself. This is not always easy.

A routine that is used many times has a very different status to those higher in the hierarchy. It is more like a basic instruction in the programming language than a large scale program component. After all the basic language commands are used many times without causing a problem. In this sense a simple minded approach to reusable software is a bottom up technique designed to extend the range of commands in the language. Equally clear from this point of view is the danger of modifying these low level routines - after all would you dare to change the way a basic language instruction works?

Finally, as structure diagrams are never refined down to the level of individual instructions and as reused routines behave like language extensions, there is an argument for not showing them in structure diagrams at all! Of course this is an argument that has to be tempered by common sense.

Hierarchy and scope

The hierarchy can tell you more than just what module calls what module. If you think for a moment about the dependency between the called and the calling module you should be able to see that information passes into a module as you move down the hierarchy and out of a module back up the hierarchy. For example, getdata might pass information into getvalue which in turn returns information to getdata but not vice versa. In other words the hierarchy determines, or rather displays, the natural flow of data within the entire program.

Some computer languages expect the programmer to take care of the flow of data up and down the hierarchy explicitly by using appropriate parameters for each module - see Chapter Three. Surprisingly some languages, usually referred to as block structured languages, try to help the programmer by way of rules - scope rules - that define the visibility of a variable.

For example, Pascal uses the scope rule that any variable declared within a procedure exists for any procedure (or block) also declared within it. The only exception is if the procedure declares a variable of the same name in which case a new local variable is created.

For example, in

```
PROGRAM main(input,output);
VAR i,j,k:INTEGER;
    PROCEDURE one;
    VAR k:INTEGER;
    BEGIN
        etc..
    END;
END.
```

the variables i,j and k are declared in the main program and so exist and can be accessed from any procedure declared within the main program. That is, if statements within PROCEDURE one make use of i or j they will use the variables that have been declared in the main program. However as PROCEDURE one declares its own variable k any references to k will be to a local variable and not the k declared in the main program which will remain unaffected by any references to PROCEDURE one's k. A reference to a variable that isn't local to a procedure is called a non-local reference. The scope rules constitute a sort of halfway house between local and global variables. A variable is local to the block that it is declared in, but global to any blocks that are nested within it.

It is clear that Pascal's scope rules are designed to follow the natural flow of information up and down the module hierarchy. Strangely many Pascal programmers don't seem to be aware of this fact. For example, if you have four procedures making up the following hierarchy

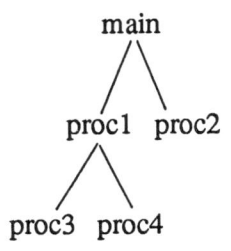

```
            main
           /    \
       proc1    proc2
       /   \
    proc3  proc4
```

then you could declare them properly nested as in

```
PROGRAM main(input,output);
  PROCEDURE proc1;
   PROCEDURE proc3;
   BEGIN
    ... body of proc3
   END;
   PROCEDURE proc4;
   BEGIN
       ... body of proc4
   END;
   BEGIN
    ... body of proc1
   END;
   PROCEDURE proc2;
   BEGIN
    ... body of proc2
   END;
   BEGIN
    ... body of main program
   END.
```

(Notice that lines have been added to the program to indicate where one procedure starts and another ends.) In this case any variables declared in proc1 would be accessible in proc3 and proc4 unless variables of the same name were declared locally. Many Pascal programmers would simply define each of the procedures within the main program

```
PROGRAM main(input,output);
  PROCEDURE proc4;
    ...
  PROCEDURE proc3;
    ...
  PROCEDURE proc1;
    ...
  PROCEDURE proc2;
    ...
END.
```

In this case only the variables declared within the main program are global to the procedures. The reason for the strange order of declaration is simply that by default Pascal only allows backward references to identifiers. So proc4 and proc3 have to be defined before proc1 to allow it to call them without generating a 'procedure undefined' error. Notice that in the properly nested version the procedures are automatically ordered so that a forward reference cannot occur.

I suppose at this point you are wondering which version of the snippet of Pascal is correct? The answer is ... it all depends. There are some programmers of the opinion that Pascal's scope rules are very dangerous and encourage sloppy programming. There are those who think that they are marvellous and any language which doesn't use them is primitive. Personally I don't like the idea of global variables in any form, but I have to admit that Pascal's scope rules are sophisticated enough for me to want to make an exception.

While we are on the subject of Pascal declarations, I might as well add that the strange idea of writing all of the procedures that the main program (or a procedure) uses before the body of the program has always seemed the wrong way around to me! I like my programs to be laid out

>   main program
>   procedures

rather than Pascal's 'procedures over programs' way of

>   procedures
>   main program

The reason why I find this awkward is that I imagine the module hierarchy as a tree diagram that grows down and not up the page! The only reason that this method was adopted was to make it easier to write a one-pass Pascal compiler!

I suppose the ideal way of laying out the hierarchical structure of a program would be to use a **hypertext** editor. This would initially show the main program until the user pointed and clicked on a subroutine name when that subroutine would be displayed. In this way you could travel up and down the hierarchy in a natural way.

Breaking the structure

If a program is working properly then the hierarchy shows the way that one module calls another and the return sequence. For example, in the hierarchy diagram at the start of the chapter it is obvious that the main program calls getdata which in turn calls message. When message finishes, control is returned to getdata which then calls getvalue. When getvalue finishes, control is returned to getdata and then on back up the hierarchy to the main program and so on..

This hierarchical call and return sequence is the proper behaviour of the program when everything is working as expected. It represents the programmer's plan to deal with the norm. But what if things aren't the norm? For example, suppose the main program calls initial and because the data supplied by the user were a little strange it is discovered that the remainder of the calculation cannot be performed? Typical situations of this sort are division by zero, no data supplied, values too large or too small, singular matrices, impossible values etc.. Whatever the reason, the situation represents an exception to the normal behaviour of the program because now there is no point in following the remaining call and return sequence. There is no point in initial returning control to workout to then call iterate because there is no hope of completing the calculation. Indeed it would be a waste of time and possibly misleading to go on to follow the normal execution of the program to the results phase.

Clearly what is needed here is some way of ignoring the hierarchy and returning control back up to the main program, or even back to the input data section of the program. You can think of this as a need to make a transfer of control to some point in the hierarchy without any regard to the structure of the program.

There are programmers who think that this view of handling exceptional situations by abandoning the hierarchy is just sloppy programming. You could just as easily build in a proper test for the exception and a normal section of code to deal with it. In other words as long as you prepare for an exception it becomes a normal part of the program's functioning and it isn't an exception any more! The argument is a long and difficult one. I for one feel that a program's behaviour is different when something occurs to stop its normal functioning and in that sense the idea of exception handling does correspond to the way at least one programmer thinks about things. The best way to imagine it is to think of starting from scratch to design a program that works in the error situation. This would have a structure similar, but not identical, to the original program. The problem is that when the error occurs you somehow need to transform the structure of the original program to that of the error handler. The alternative view is that as the two structures are similar it should be possible to produce a single structure that reflects both situations.

Various languages do include methods of handling exceptions, Ada, PL/1 and BASIC for example, but to my mind none have the anything like an answer to the problem of finding yourself deep in a hierarchy and suddenly wanting to transform it into a different structure. The Ada exception is described further in Chapter Eight. We have spent the past fifty or so years looking into the design of programs that work perfectly in ideal conditions - perhaps now is the time to consider the production of programs that work no matter what is thrown at them, be it expected or unexpected.

key points

- Modular programs tend to be hierarchical.

- This hierarchy can be exploited to control the construction of programs and to make their description easier.

- Stepwise refinement is a simple top down programming method that aids program assembly.

- Real programming methods are generally neither top down nor bottom up.

- Block structured scope rules aid the flow of information up and down the hierarchy but at the expense of introducing global variables.

- When an error occurs the normal structure of the program may be inappropriate. Modern languages include facilities for handling such exceptions.

Chapter Five
Data = type + structure

The first skill that you have to acquire as a programmer is the ability to understand how something is done and convert it into an exact description i.e. a program. At first all of the problems that you meet are concerned with this translation from real world process to a static written form. Later on it becomes apparent that a second skill is needed - the ability to convert real world objects into representations that the program can operate on. It is a funnelling of reality into the machine where a program can get to work on it. Clearly the quality of such a representation is critical to the ease of program construction. It may even limit what can be done.

The role of data

The obvious importance of data leads many programmers to claim that data representation is more fundamental to the programmer's art than anything else. I don't think that this is true because it is a skill that can only develop after a great many others have been mastered. In this sense it is this skill that differentiates between a good and a great programmer. You have to master the nitty gritty detail of loops, selects and even all of the theory about data structures before you can even begin to think about how the abstract data inside the machine has anything to do with the outside world.

In other words, data representation is important but you have to reach a certain level of skill before being able to reflect on this importance. You could almost say that early in their programming career programmers consider their work as being wholly contained within the machine and only later do they see the relationship with the outside world. For example typical first year programming assignments are nearly always described in computer terms as in 'write a program to reverse the order of a list of numbers' and very rarely in non-computer terms as in 'a factory needs to keep a stock level of items...' You can see that the list of numbers is already a computer object, an array, thinly disguised. The problem has been constructed by thinking about programming and selecting a topic rather than looking at the external world.

The reason for working within the computer world at this early stage is reasonable because the real world generally produces problems that are too difficult for the beginner to tackle in a short time. The danger is that the beginner may never develop the skill of translating real world objects into computer world objects. In this case they remain trapped in the task of extending and improving other programmer's ideas.

As in the case of programming in general most data representations are constructed out of known fragments. You need a toolkit of basic data representation techniques so that you can identify the best representation for any new problem and perhaps even so that you can recognise something new when you see it. Later in this chapter you will find a brief synopsis of the standard types of data which should be enough for you to fill in the details of implementation for yourself.

A very popular view of the role of data is that it is the static object that the process of the program works on. The expression made familiar by Wirth 'Algorithms+Data Structures = Programs' captures this idea very well. You could also say that the data structures are the nouns and the control structures are the verbs of a program. To a certain extent this view overemphasises the distinction between the data object and the operations that are associated with it. It may be that to make progress we have to think more of the data object as something that is active in its own right. This is the approach taken by object oriented programming.

Fundamental types

An experienced programmer should have come across many different types of data in the course of constructing programs. Without an exposure to the raw material of representing things inside a computer you can't begin to make progress on the more subtle and interesting task of choosing a good representation. For the sake of completeness, and to form a sort of checklist of things that every programmer should know, it is worth giving a description of the basic types of data from which everything else is built.

If you bother to go all the way back to the origins of it all then the data in our programs, indeed the programs themselves, are nothing more than a pattern of voltage levels inside the machine. Most programmers are happy enough to think of these voltage levels as standing for two symbols usually chosen to be 0 and 1. Hence data representation is a matter of making patterns or **bit strings** from these basic symbols. Even this point of view is a little too primitive for most, and high level languages generally try to hide this level by treating the patterns of 0 and 1 as integers. No doubt as time goes on the underlying bit patterns will be forgotten and the integer will be regarded as fundamental! At this stage in our development there are still languages, C, Fortran 66 and some dialects of BASIC, where the bit string lurks just beneath the surface. For many reasons there is still a need for a programmer to know about bit strings, Boolean logic, and binary and other base representations.

The bit string is used to represent data by simple positional coding. Each position in the bit string is assigned a meaning and the bit is used to code a simple presence/absence state. For example, if your computer is controlling the lights in your house then each bit might be assigned to a particular light and its 0/1 state corresponds to on/off. You can see that a single bit can be used to represent two states. To represent more states you need more bits. Two bits can represent four states, three bits eight and so on. For example, if the light has four levels of brightness I could assign two bits and use the code 00=off, 01=dim, 10=bright, 11=full on. This sort of coding may seem simple but it is worth remembering that everything in programming is built from it!

86 Data = type + structure Chapter Five

It is usual to move on quickly from such codings to consider how bit strings can be used to represent numbers. This is achieved by a slight extension to the coding principle. To represent a number positional weights are added to the bit string. The most usual system of weights corresponds to the binary system. That is the weights are 1, 2, 4, 8, 16 etc. so the bit string 01011001 represents 89 (decimal).

weight	128	64	32	16	8	4	2	1	
bit string	0	1	0	1	1	0	0	1	
total	0	64	0	16	8	0	0	1	= 89

You can see that this scheme only allows positive integers to be represented but it is easy to extend it to include negative integers and fractional numbers. It is important to realise that although this form of representation is amazingly convenient and as a result almost universally used it isn't the only one possible. For example you can assign the weights 1, 2, 4, 8, 10, 20, 40, 80, 100, 200, 400, 800 etc. to produce the system usually called **BCD** (Binary Coded Decimal). In this system the same bit string represents 59

weight	80	40	20	10	8	4	2	1	
bit string	0	1	0	1	1	0	0	1	
total	0	40	0	10	8	0	0	1	=59

Notice that in this coding each group of four bits can be read as a decimal digit using standard binary coding i.e. 0101 = 5 and 1001=9. This accounts for the extra condition usually imposed on a BCD representation, to avoid the fact that some values can be represented in more than one way, that each group of four bits must represent a value less than 10 in simple binary.

Having gone so far into bit strings and representations it is worth mentioning that the negative integers are generally represented using **twos complement**. This scheme uses the same binary weights but with the highest value treated as negative. Twos complement numbers often remain a complete mystery to student programmers but seen as just another bit string coding they are easy. For example in this scheme the bit string 11011001 represents -39.

weight	-128	64	32	16	8	4	2	1	
bit string	1	1	0	1	1	0	0	1	
total	-128	64	0	16	8	0	0	1	= -39

Although bit strings are more fundamental, the movement to higher levels of abstraction, i.e. taking us further away from the underlying machine, is favouring the view that integers are about as fundamental as you need to get. Perhaps in years to come programmers will be spared the need to study binary!

Integer and real

There are only two different types of basic data in most languages - **integers** and **real** numbers. All of the other supplied data types are constructed from the integers. The real numbers are special in that, apart from complex numbers, they don't lend themselves to forming other basic types of data.

Integers are just whole positive or negative numbers. In any programming language or computer system integers are generally restricted to a given range of values. This range depends on the number of bits allocated to storing an integer. The more bits the bigger the range but the more memory used and the slower the arithmetic operations involving them. So in principle the only programming problem inherent in using integers is the possibility of exceeding the legal range or in assuming a legal range that is illegal on another computer. Many languages provide a constant, such as MAXINT in Pascal, that can be used to test that an integer is in the legal range. It is also common for languages to provide integers of different size and hence range. For example, Fortran provides a notation to determine the amount of storage to be used for an integer. INTEGER*1 used 1 storage allocation, INTEGER*2 used 2 and so on. However in any given system not all sizes of integer are made available and the upper limit is usually INTEGER*4. Similarly C and Ada provide long and short integers in addition to standard integers. Ada also allows the programmer to define the range that is legal for an integer variable and it will automatically select the best machine representation.

Real numbers are differ from integers in having a fractional part. (The term 'real' has its origins in mathematics and has nothing to do with the reality of the numbers concerned!) Originally real numbers were implemented as **fixed point** values. This corresponds to simply treating an integer as if it has so many digits after the decimal point. For example, the integer 123456 might be regarded as the fixed point number 123.456. Fixed point numbers are very inefficient and don't provide the numeric range required by most calculations. These days a **floating point** representation is more common, indeed real and floating point are taken to mean the same thing in most languages.

A floating point value is represented in two parts - the mantissa which holds the most significant digits and the exponent which determines the magnitude of the number. To be more precise the floating point constant 1.45E5 is equal to $1.45*10^5$ which is 1.45*100000 or 145000. Negative exponents correspond to numbers smaller than one. In different systems varying amounts of storage are allocated to the exponent and the mantissa. The more bits allocated to the exponent the greater the range of numbers that can be represented and the more bits allocated to the mantissa the greater the precision. Notice that when using floating point representation there is a smallest number that can be represented as well as a largest.

The biggest difference between real values and integers is that real value computations are imprecise. This often doesn't matter as long as the number of meaningful digits in an answer is sufficient for the purpose. The whole question of numerical accuracy in computation is complicated and more a matter for the numerical analyst than the programmer. However there is one general programming problem caused by real values - testing for equality. If you are comparing the result of two real calculations for equality then lack of precision will tend to ruin the attempt. For example, if you are trying to end a loop using

IF x=y THEN ...

and x and y are real values then, even if theory tells you that they should be equal at some point during the repeated calculation, the chances are that lack of precision will make sure that they never are exactly equal in practice. The solution to this problem is well known but often forgotten. You should avoid comparing real values for equality wherever possible and use greater than or less than tests instead. That is use

IF x=>y THEN ..

If a test for equality cannot be converted in this way then the only alternative is to use a test for approximate equality as in

IF x-y<tol THEN..

where tol (for tolerance) is a very small number roughly equally to the precision that you are working to.

The only numeric type that is built up from real variables is the complex type. The only language that supports complex numbers directly is Fortran but procedures and functions for manipulating complex numbers are easy enough to provide in modern languages such as Ada and Modula-2. Even so the availability of COMPLEX in Fortran might account for much of its continuing popularity with scientists and engineers.

Scalar types

Both integer and real numbers are examples of **scalar** data. The term scalar comes from physics where it means a quantity without an associated direction i.e. something that isn't a vector. There are other scalars but these can all built up from integers. The most common standard scalars are **Boolean**, i.e two values true and false, and characters. The Boolean type is often explicitly implemented as an integer using 0 as false and -1 (say) as true. Surprisingly Fortran 66 did a good job of covering up how Boolean values were represented in its LOGICAL type but stored characters as integers! Most languages provide special variable types and facilities for handling characters but most programmers know that they are represented by their ASCII or some other standard code value. In fact the main problem caused by character data is the non-standard way that the integers are associated with characters. For example, what is the ASCII code for a pound sign?

As well as the supplied scalar types modern languages usually allow the programmer to define their own scalar types. For example, in Pascal, Ada and Modula-2 you can define an **enumerated** type for the days of the week using

TYPE days=(sun,mon,tue,wed,thr,fri,sat)

Following this you can declare variables of this type and the only values that you can store in such variables are sun, mon, tue etc.. Similarly you can define **subranges** of existing types as in

TYPE dayno=1..365

following which you can declare variables of the type dayno and only assign values in the range 1 to 365 to them.

When you first see enumerated types they look very clever but it doesn't take long to see that all that is happening is a renaming and restriction in range of the integer type. In other words in the days of the week example sun is assigned to 0, mon to 1 and so on. You can achieve more or less the same effect in more primitive languages manually by assigning values to variables or constants, as in sun=0, mon=1 etc.. Following this you can write assignments such as workday=mon.

The main difference between a proper enumerated type and the manual method is that the language usually restricts the sort of operation you are allowed to perform on enumerated types. For example, workday+1 would be illegal if workday was an enumerated type but not if it was an integer. Generally it is up to you to define functions and if the language allows operators to work on the new scalar type that you have defined. Pascal provides the functions succ and pred to enable you to find the successor and predecessor of a given enumerated type value but that's about all. For example, succ(mon)=tue and pred(thr)=wed.

Data typing

All programming languages provide a range of fundamental data types - integers, reals, characters etc.. Some languages take the attitude that all data types are logically separate and as such they should be kept separate. This approach is called **strong typing** and languages such as Pascal and Modula-2 force programmers to declare the type of a variable before it is used. (To be precise the term strong typing implies that any type violations can be discovered just by examining the program text i.e. at compile time and in this sense Pascal isn't quite a strongly typed language.) After a type declaration different types are kept apart and you cannot assign the contents of one type to another. The argument goes that assigning a character variable to an integer is like mixing apples with oranges and should be flagged as an error. This seems reasonable until you enforce it on ALL variable types. It seems much less of a crime to assign an integer to a real or a string of length 5 to a string of length 6. If you think that making a distinction between strings of different length is taking it a bit far then I would agree but then this is exactly what Modula-2 does! In practice however even the most strongly typed languages tend to relax their compatibility rules to make life tolerable.

At the other end of the range there are languages that attempt to remove any restrictions on using one type of data with another. In such a language an assignment between one data type and another would bring about a type conversion without the user knowing anything about it. For example, BASIC is a fairly type free language but it still insists on the use of special functions if you want to assign a character to an integer i.e. C=ASC(A$) but there is no reason why you couldn't be allowed to write C=A$ and expect the language to take care of the conversion! I don't think I have ever come across a completely type-free language but languages such as Lisp and Logo make a good attempt.

There are a variety of reasons put forward for either using or not using data typing. The most common is that data typing forces a programmer to define all variables and their type before using them and this is a good discipline. In addition it stops programmers from making mistakes by assigning one type of data to another. This is a sort of not adding oranges to apples principle. However an important reason for not supporting the free assignment of one type of data to another is that it is difficult to implement. Many language features are determined by what is easy for the compiler writer to implement and this isn't an unreasonable situation. What is unreasonable is that many programmers trained using particular languages often accept the features that they find as being examples of the best possible world. It can be hard to look at something that you know well and have grown to love and see its faults!

After looking at a range of languages I think that the broad argument for data typing is a good one but it shouldn't be applied as a rigorous mathematical principle. Doing this leads to ridiculous situations where assigning an integer to a real is impossible and a string of three characters is distinctly different from a string of two characters. Data should be typed into wide categories - numbers, truth values, text etc.. and there should be simple but explicit methods of converting one type to another. For example, while I would object to having to write a=FLOAT(i) explicitly to convert the integer i to a real, I don't have the same unease about a$=CHR$(i) to explicitly convert an integer to a character.

Languages that do not insist on conversion functions generally operate default type conversion rules. This process is often called **type coercion**. It operates by defining a hierarchy of types such that any type lower in the hierarchy can be converted into a higher type without loss of information. For example an integer can be converted into a real without loss of information but not vice versa - the fractional part would be lost. Type coercion is used to convert all data types involved in an expression into the highest type used in the expression before it is evaluated. Occasionally type coercion doesn't give the desired result and in this case the programmer is forced to use explicit conversion or **transfer functions** as they are called. Type coercion can make a program look simpler but it can also be used to implement devious tricks. As always clarity is most important and there are times when an explicit transfer function should be used, even if the language allows default type conversion, just to draw attention to exactly what is going on.

Basic static structures

Once you have met the fundamental data types the next stage is to look at ways of structuring them. A **data structuring** method is simply a way of organising the fundamental data types to produce something new. You have to provide the rule for organising the fundamental data types and rules for selecting one or more of their number. This is a very abstract definition that becomes much clearer once you have seen a few structured data types - mainly the array and the record.

There is no need to introduce the idea of a structuring method, as distinct from real data structures such as the array etc. You could, and many introductory courses do, simply define new data types such as the array as and when they were required. However there is an advantage to be gained from seeing this as part of a grand design rather than a one off event. For example, once you see that the process of grouping together a single data type and allowing access to it by an index is general, and doesn't depend on the underlying data type you can see that the structuring method can be applied to anything including other structured types. So a two dimensional array can be seen as an array of one dimensional arrays, you can have arrays of records, arrays of files, records of arrays etc..

The array

The first data structure that we all meet is the **array.** Indeed it is usual to meet the array even before the complete range of fundamental data types. An array is a collection of variables of the same type indexed by a variable of another type. In nearly all languages the index type is integer (or real converted to integer) but this is not necessary. For example, the language Snobol allows arrays indexed by strings so you can use expressions like WEEK("MON")=3.6 to mean assign 3.6 to the array element of WEEK indexed by "MON".

Arrays are so well known by most programmers that there is no need to labour the point. However if you have only used languages such as BASIC or Fortran 66 then you might not realise the flexibility that other languages provide. The main difference comes from allowing the lower as well as upper limit on the array index to be declared. For example, the BASIC statement

DIM a(10)

creates an array with 11 elements a(0) to a(10) but in Pascal you can write statements like

VAR a: ARRAY [5..8] OF integer

which creates an array of four elements a[5] to a[8]. This is a useful convenience that does avoid messy index expressions, but it isn't essential. For example, in BASIC a four element array a(0) to a(3) can be accessed as if it was indexed a(5) to a(8) by using the index expression a(i-5). You should be able to see that when i is five the element accessed is a(0) and so on. Modern versions of BASIC, such as Quick and Turbo BASIC allow you to specify upper and lower limits on an array.

Arrays and enumeration loops were made for each other. The main use of an enumeration loop is in stepping through the elements of an array. As long as you can write a loop that generates the correct values of the index variable then this is easy. For example, to print array elements in reverse order in BASIC is easy

```
FOR i=n TO 0 STEP -1
    PRINT a(i)
NEXT i
```

But in Fortran 66 the step size must be positive and so an index expression has to be used

```
      DO 1 i=1,n,1
         WRITE(5,2)a(n-i+1)
    1 CONTINUE
```

This problem, coupled with arrays that always start from 1, forced Fortran programmers to be good at index expressions!

The only other detail worth mentioning about arrays is more to do with subroutine implementation than data structure. In most languages you can pass an array to a subroutine along with a parameter that gives its size. This allows subroutines that can perform a task on a general array to be written. However the original version of Pascal insisted that an array's size was known before the program or subroutine was run and so a subroutine for each size of array was necessary. Thankfully this limitation has been removed in ISO Pascal and most modern languages.

Once you have the idea of an array you can introduce arrays of two and more dimensions. Some languages treat such multidimensional arrays as arrays of one dimensional arrays. For example, in Pascal a two dimensional array can be defined using

    VAR a :ARRAY [1..10] OF ARRAY [1..10] OF integer

or

    VAR a:ARRAY [1..10,1..10] OF integer

In each case the result is a two-dimensional array a[i,j]. In the same way you can write array elements either as a[i,j] or as a[i][j]. The second way emphasises the array of arrays nature of the two-dimensional array. That is a[i] is an element that is itself a one-dimensional array from which [j] then selects a single element.

Treating a two-dimensional array as an array of arrays has the advantage that the component arrays can be split out and used where appropriate. For example, if max(x) is a procedure that finds the maximum of a one-dimensional array you could use max(a[i]) to find the maximum of the ith column of the two-dimensional array a[i,j]. Some languages also permit the use of operators and functions on arrays or part of arrays without the need to use explicit loops. For example, in APL you can write

    a <- 2*a

which if a is an array (vector in APL) has the same effect as

    FOR i=1 TO n
        a(i)=2*a(i)
    NEXT i

As Ada allows functions to return results that are arrays or records you can implement the same sort of array operations and even write them as operators. Ada also supports an array slice notation. For example, a(4..8)=b(5..9) will assign b(5) to a(4) and so on to b(9) to a(8). However all of this is the exception and most languages still expect you to perform array operations using explicit loops.

The record

A **record** (called a structure in C) can be thought of as an array of mixed elements. For example, you could have a record composed of a string of characters and two numeric variables and its definition in Pascal would be

```
TYPE EMPLOY = RECORD
    NAME:STRING;
    AGE:INTEGER;
    PAY:REAL;
END;
```

and you could gain access to its elements or **fields** by using qualified names. For example, EMPLOY.NAME="JONES", EMPLOY.AGE=64, EMPLOY.PAY=0. Notice that the second part of the name .NAME, .AGE and .PAY, acts just like the index variable in an array. The difference is that, while an index value can be computed, a field name has to be explicitly written in the program. As a result there is no natural control structure for the record in the way that the FOR loop works with the array. This means that programs that manipulate records are very long and wordy. Fortunately most record operations are just a matter of moving fields from one place to another, updating fields and testing fields. Even though these operations are simple they tend to be repetitive in a way that cannot be automated using a loop. Database programs, even those written in a database language such as dBASE, are thus unique in being simple in principle but a complex mass of fieldnames and almost, but not quite, identical expressions.

Data Structures

Array
a

a(i)

An array of identical elements. A single element is selected by the value of the index.

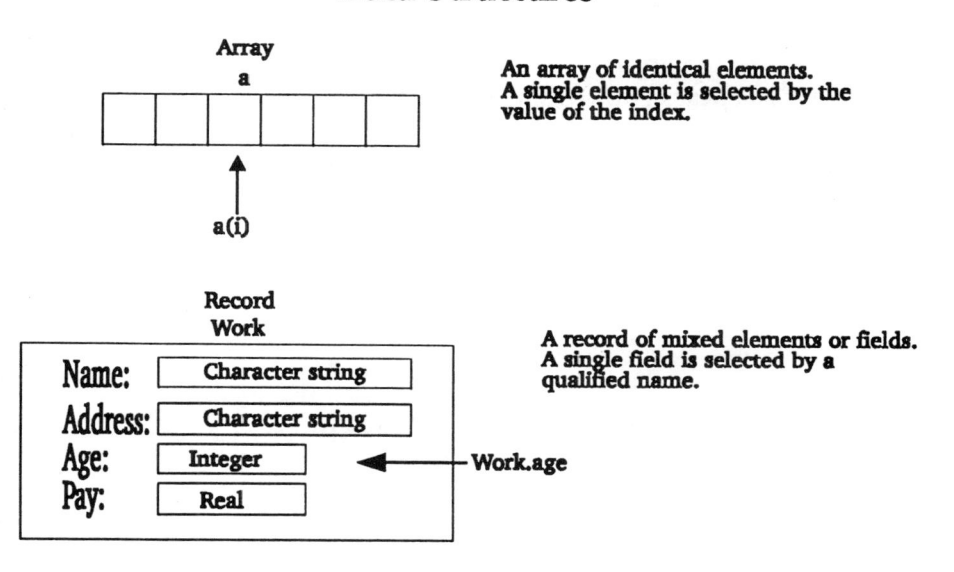

Record
Work

Name:	Character string
Address:	Character string
Age:	Integer
Pay:	Real

← Work.age

A record of mixed elements or fields. A single field is selected by a qualified name.

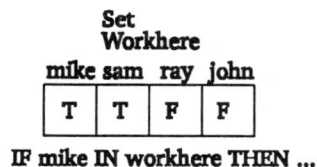

Set
Workhere

mike	sam	ray	john
T	T	F	F

IF mike IN workhere THEN ...

A set of elements is equivalent to a Boolean array indicating presence or absence of each element in the set.

A file is a sequential list of items. One item can be read or written at a time and the file pointer is adjusted automatically.

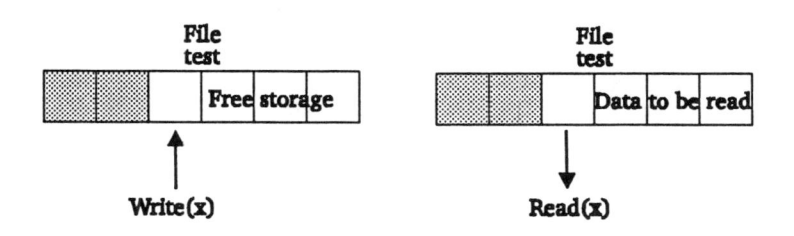

File
test

			Free	storage

↑
Write(x)

File
test

		Data	to be	read

↓
Read(x)

The set

The **set** is a very simple, but if you have never met it before a potentially confusing, data structure. A set is an unordered collection of items. Each item can appear in the set only once. If the same item can appear more than once then the structure is called a **bag**. Sets are available as standard in Pascal and Modula-2 and they can be created with little difficulty in Ada.

Sets behave as program equivalents of mathematical sets and come complete with standard set theory operations. For example, in Pascal the statements

> TYPE people=(mike, sam, ray, john);
> VAR workhere:SET OF people;
> workhere=[mike,sam]

create workhere as a set of people and then assigns the set consisting of mike and sam to it. You can test to see if an element is contained in a set, test to see if one set is a subset of another, add new elements, combine sets by set union and set intersection, etc..

The way that sets work becomes easier to understand once you know how they are usually implemented. The variable workhere can be implemented as an array of Boolean type. Each element records the presence or absence of an item in the set. For example, after the assignment workhere=[mike,sam] the array would contain

mike	sam	ray	john
T	T	F	F

where T stands for True and F for False. Seen in this light sets are nothing more than an appropriate high level abstraction of a bit pattern and can be used for the same range of tasks.

Files

One of the most important data structures in practice is the **sequential file** and its more powerful relation, the **direct access** file. Most programmers know how sequential files behave but usually treat them as something different and in some way external to the program. This attitude is reinforced by the way that most high level languages assume that files are to do with the operating system and rarely provide adequate commands for handling them. Pascal does at least recognise the fact that a file is just another data structure and allows files of any base type (apart from a file) to be declared. For example

> VAR text:FILE OF char

declares a text to be a sequential file of characters. A sequential file is usually used via appropriate functions to store or retrieve data. Only one data item can be stored or retrieved at a time and items are retrieved in the same order that they were stored in. This is usually thought of as reading and writing data at a location in the file indicated by a pointer. When writing the file the pointer is automatically incremented to point at a free storage location. When reading the file the pointer is automatically incremented to point at the next data item.

The only difference between a sequential file and a direct access file is that data can be read and written in any order. This is usually implemented in high level languages by providing a statement to explicitly set the file pointer. Of course this leaves it up to the programmer to create more complex and useful file organisations that make it possible to find any given item of data quickly.

Dynamic data

The next stage is to begin to look at the so called dynamic data structures. These are called dynamic because they have the potential to change their size and configuration as a program runs. The best known dynamic structures are the stacks - Last In First Out and First In First Out, the queue, the deque - a double ended queue, linear lists and trees and graphs of all varieties. If you want a detailed description of each of these data types then consult any good book on data structures. However it is still worth making a few comments about the best known types.

The LIFO stack

A LIFO (Last In First Out) stack is often used as a way of altering the order that data items are processed in. A LIFO stack has two associated operations PUSH and PULL. A PUSH operation stores a data item on the top of the stack and a PULL operation retrieves an item from the top of the stack. For example, following PUSH(a), PUSH(b), PUSH(c) a PULL operation will retrieve c, then b and then a. You can see that as the data was pushed in the order a,b,c and retrieved in the order c,b,a a stack can be used to reverse a sequence of data. Another way of looking at this is to say that a stack delivers up data items 'freshest first'. In practice it is this order reversal property which is important and it can be used in some surprisingly powerful ways. For example, a stack can be used to evaluate operator expressions taking into account operator precedence and brackets.

The FIFO stack or queue

Once you have seen a LIFO stack then the FIFO (First In First Out) stack is an obvious modification. This retrieves data in the order that it was stored in. A FIFO stack is also called a queue because you can imagine data items queuing up waiting their turn to be processed. A queue is naturally associated with two operations usually called JOIN, i.e. store a data item at the end of the queue, and LEAVE, i.e. retrieve a data item from the front of the queue. Queues are relatively boring when compared to LIFO stacks and mainly serve as buffers for data that cannot be processed fast enough or to simulate queues in the real world.

The double ended queue or deque

A double ended queue is simply a FIFO stack but with two extra operations that allows data to join at the front of the queue and leave at the back. You can think of a double ended queue as a normal queue but with pushing in and queue jumping! Another name for a double ended queue is a deque - inspired by the image of dealing from the top and bottom of a deck of cards. A less fanciful name is dequeue from double ended queue.

Dynamic data structures

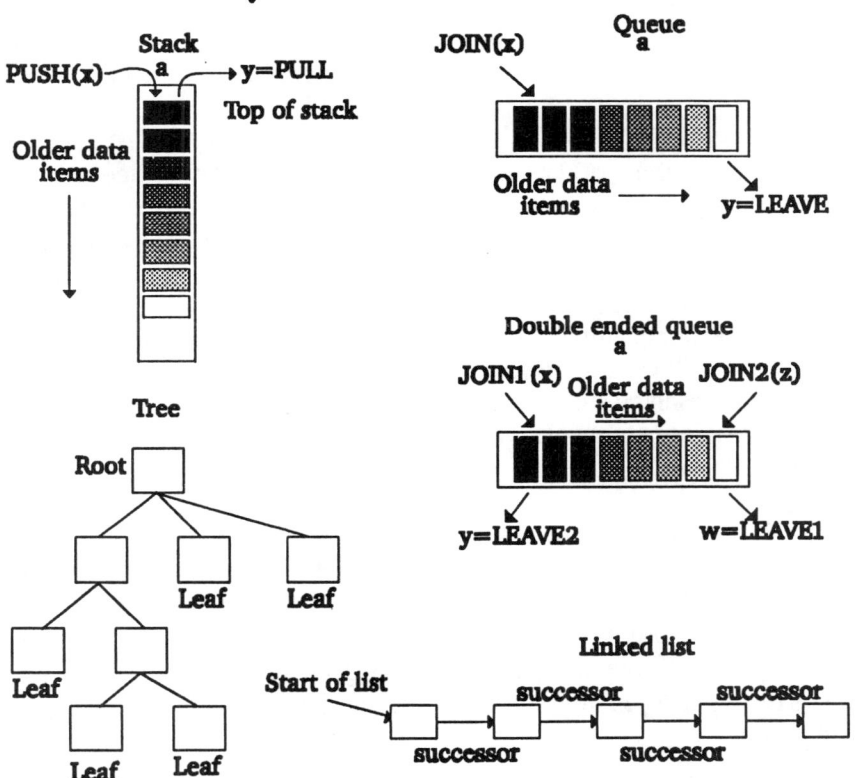

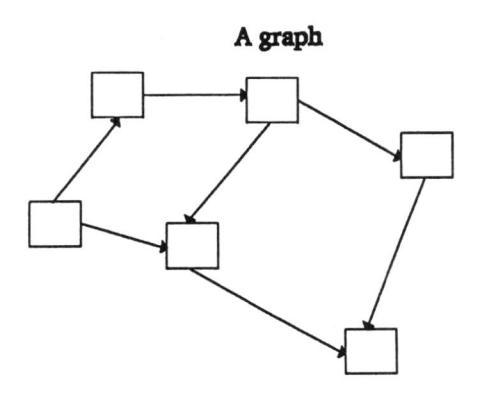

Stack

PUSH(x) → a → y=PULL
Top of stack

Older data items ↓

Queue a

JOIN(x) →

Older data items → y=LEAVE

Double ended queue a

JOIN1(x) Older items JOIN2(z)

y=LEAVE2   w=LEAVE1

Tree

Root — Leaf — Leaf — Leaf — Leaf — Leaf

Linked list

Start of list → successor → successor → successor → successor

A graph

The linked list
This is a list of data items in which each item has a successor. The successor of the current item can always be found but moving back though the list can be more difficult. To get round this problem some lists include a successor and a predecessor link to enable movement in both directions through the list. Such a list is usually called a **doubly linked list**.

The tree
A tree is a hierarchy of data items. One data item starts the tree off and for obvious reasons is called the root. Each item in the tree can have a number of descendants. An item that has no descendent is a terminal or leaf item. The idea of a tree is very simple but there are many different special forms of tree that are arrived at by some restriction on the more general idea. For example, a binary tree is one in which each item has two descendants. Trees are important data structures whenever a hierarchy has to be represented and also when data can be organised into a hierarchy to make searching more efficient.

The graph
A graph can be though of as a generalisation of a tree. Each item in a graph has a number of successors, which may even be items that occurred earlier in the structure. An alternative name for a graph is a network and this is more descriptive of the 'shape' of the data structure. Graphs are mainly used to represent real world networks. As with trees there are many different types of graph that are essentially restricted types of the full graph.

Implementing dynamic types - pointers

A dynamic data structure is usually created by using pointers but there are a few other methods that apply in special cases. A pointer is a variable that can be used to store the identity of another variable. There is a tendency to think in terms of a pointer as storing the address of the variable but this is just an echo of the way that the hardware works. Once you have a pointer data type you can use it to link data structures together in whatever pattern you like and determine the position in a data structure at which the next item will be stored. For example, you can make a linear list of records by declaring the final field as a pointer. The list is built up using the pointer to store the identity of the next record. Once you have the idea you can make the linear list as complicated as you like by adding additional pointers to the previous record, to the start of the list, to the end of the list and so on.

As well as linking data structures together pointers can be used to indicate where data should be stored. This is used to implement dynamic data structures such as stacks. For example, if you declare a pointer to the start of a structure, an array say, then this is where data is stored during a PUSH operation. Of course the pointer would be adjusted following every PUSH operation to indicate the next free location ready for the next PUSH. A PULL operation would be implemented in more or less the same way apart from the pointer being adjusted to point to the previously free location.

Most programming languages provide pointers to enable you to construct your own dynamic data structures. In practice it is a good idea to adopt the information hiding approach to create a new data type complete with its associated operations. For example, instead of just using an array and an index variable to implement a stack, it is better to create a procedure push(x) and a function x=pull to manipulate the stack and keep the details of implementation hidden.

When are types equal?

A problem that is created by taking a hard line attitude to data typing is 'when are two types equal?' It is clear that an integer isn't the same type as a character but when you can create structured types life isn't so simple. For example, it is clear that the arrays x and y declared by

VAR x,y:ARRAY [1..10] OF integer

are the same and should be treated as such. However it turns out to be quite difficult to tell in general if two variables are of the same type if they aren't declared at the same time. Two variables that are identical in structure are said to be **structure equivalent**. However most languages use **name equivalence** to determine when two types are the same. What this amounts to is that two variables either have to be declared in the same statement or using the same type name for them to be considered equal. For example, the statements

>TYPE big = array [1..10] OF integer;
>VAR x:big;
>VAR y:big;

defines two variables of the same type as does

>VAR x,y:ARRAY [1..10] OF integer;

but

>VAR x:ARRAY [1..10] OF integer;
>VAR y:ARRAY [1..10] OF integer

defines two variables of different type! This is clearly not a satisfactory situation.

Strings

A very important dynamic data type that deserves consideration on its own is the string. In most languages, including Pascal, Ada, Modula-2 and C, a string of characters is treated as a fixed size character array. For example

>VAR c:ARRAY [1..25] OF char

is the best that Pascal can do in representing a string of characters. This is not a good data structure for dealing with text because it imposes the condition that exactly 25 characters will always be used.

A more realistic string data structure has been available in BASIC for many years. In BASIC a string is a variable length data item that will store however many characters are assigned to it (up to some large practical limit). For example, in BASIC a$="hello" is perfectly valid without declaring that a$ is a string of a particular size and you can assign any number of characters to a$ at any time. String operations are available by way of functions to extract and manipulate sub-strings and comparison operations are performed on strings of unequal length in a perfectly sensible way. The main reason why these facilities haven't been made available in other languages is efficiency. It is difficult to implement dynamic strings without using excessive storage or slowing the program down to an unacceptable level. Some languages, C for example, compromise by using a fixed length array of characters in combination with an 'end of string' marker to allow for strings shorter than this declared length.

Once you have used a variable length string data type it is difficult to return to the constraints and over-fussy operations that result from fixed length strings. It is one of the main reasons why BASIC was, and is, a popular language - surely other languages will follow in time.

Real v imaginary

After looking at the basic principles of data types and structures it is time to look at the wider role that data plays. One of the main reasons why it is difficult to come to grips with data is that it is not until you tackle complex problems that the real world makes an appearance. As already mentioned, when you are first learning about programming the problems are usually phrased in terms of the internal data structure that you are going to use - even if this is well hidden! For example, adding up lists of numbers or even manipulating character strings is more about working with things that are already inside the computer than anything in the real world. Even when things promise to be more complicated many programs are designed after the data representation has been decided. For example, you might want to write a program that processes a data file of records. In this case the records are internal computer objects but once upon a time someone must have decided how the information that each record holds should be stored. If you inherit someone else's choice of data structure then there is very little that you can do about it apart from get on with the job of writing the program. Every now and again though you will find yourself in the position of having to write a program from scratch and then it is up to you to make a good choice.

My main problem in going on to discuss how this choice is made is that many programmers don't think about such things at a conscious level. They certainly make a choice, and it may even be a consistently good choice of data structure, but the process that they use is more like divine inspiration than a programming method. The only way to get away from the transcendental meditation school of programming is to look at an example.

The traffic light problem

Your task is to write a program that simulates the workings of a set of traffic lights at a junction. If you don't like the idea of simulating traffic lights then imagine that problem is to control a real set of lights - the difference is just a matter of hardware. The most important question to be answered is how to represent the usual states of a traffic light. The well known sequence is Red, Red+Amber, Green, Amber and back to Red again. After having set this problem to a large number of programming classes I think that there are only two broad approaches - but you never know... The methods do seem to be produced according to the backgrounds, and perhaps even personality, of the programmers suggesting them.

The engineers, and other realists, tend to see the traffic light as consisting of three bulbs - Red, Amber and Green. So what could be more natural than using three similarly named variables coded so that 1 stands for ON and 0 for OFF. In a language such as Pascal, Modula, Ada or C++ there isn't even any need to adopt the 0/1 coding because you can use a user defined enumerated type. For example, following the declaration

TYPE BULB=(ON,OFF)

you can define three variables

VAR RED,AMBER,GREEN:BULB;

and write statements like RED:=ON and AMBER:=OFF. You can even write tests like IF RED=ON THEN.. You should be able to see that this sort of type declaration makes programs more readable but doesn't really add to the range of things that you can do. The idea of focusing on the three bulbs in each traffic light is fine but it gets a little complicated when you start to write the program because of the need to represent the red+amber state.

The mathematicians and abstract thinkers tend to see the traffic light as a logical object capable of being in any one of four states

state	action	lights
S1	go	green
S2	prepare to stop	amber
S3	stop	red
S4	get ready to go	red+amber

Of course in group discussion the solution doesn't come out as well formed as this table and often the word "state" doesn't make an appearance but the polished version comes with time! If this is the way that you view a traffic light then the appropriate data representation is to define a variable capable of holding one of four states. In Pascal this would be done by

TYPE LIGHT=(S1,S2,S3,S4)

but in any other language you would simply use an integer variable and the values 1,2,3 and 4. The advantages of this representation is that each traffic light corresponds to a single variable and the changing sequence corresponds to 'incrementing' the variable from S1 to S4 and then back to S1 again.

Abstractions

These two ways of representing the same thing each have advantages and disadvantages depending on the details of exactly what the program is trying to do. For example, the representation using light bulbs is easier to use when it comes to output. The reason for this is because this representation is closer to the physical reality of a traffic light, whereas the four states are almost a mathematical abstraction. The four states however are easier to use when it comes to going through the traffic light sequence and easier to use in conditional statements. If you would like to see the differences then try to write a program that prints the condition of a traffic light and takes it through the usual sequence of colours using both representations.

I have to admit that in this exercise the difference is slight but this is a small scale example - a tiny fragment of a real problem. The point is that the issue of how to represent real world things within a program is central to the construction of the program. Choose the correct representation and the program writes itself, choose the wrong one and it might become very nearly impossible, or worse very expensive! The trouble is that if you do choose the wrong representation this often doesn't show itself until very late on in the project. This is one of the reasons why programmers sometimes say that they could write the program better if they were allowed a second go at it.

A good representation

What makes one representation better than another? If I could answer that question with any certainty we would all know a lot more about programming, and the nature of intelligence, than we do! There are some general guidelines that can be used to say what a good representation might be. It is obvious that any representation should have as many properties of the real world object and these should be natural rather than forced by the program. For example, if you are writing a program that deals with the days of the week how should Monday, Tuesday etc. be represented. Two simple solutions that most programmers are familiar with are

1) represent the days of the week by string variables giving rise to statements such as

$$DAY\$="MONDAY"$$

2) represent the days of the week by integers or real numbers, 0=Monday and so on

To find out how good these representations are you have to ask how many of the properties of the real world object they possess naturally. The strings have the same name as the days of the week where the numbers do not. This means that you can quite happily use PRINT DAY$ but PRINT DAY would just yield a meaningless number. However the strings do not naturally mimic the fact that Tuesday comes after Monday and so on but the numbers do. In other words the order of 0,1..6 is the same as the days of the week but the usual sort order of Monday, Tuesday.. Sunday is not. Also numbers naturally preserve the 'next day' property as long as the 'successor' operation is taken as addition modulo 7. (Addition modulo 7 is just normal addition but with a wrap around back to 0 for numbers 7 or bigger. For example, 1+1 MOD 7=2 but 6+1 MOD 7=0 and 6+2 MOD 7=1 and so on.) That is

DAY+1 MOD 7

really is the integer for the next day, but how do you find the next day to DAY$? It can be done but you have to program it into the string representation.

So far it looks as if the numeric representation has a lot going for it but it also has some extra properties that days of the week don't have. For example, DAY1*DAY2 is a perfectly valid operation on numbers but doesn't make any sense for days! A representation should have as many properties of the real world object as possible but not extra ones that have nothing to do with it.

Notice that in the case of the numeric days of the week we also had to choose an operation that corresponded to finding the 'next day'. It is a little simple minded to just concentrate on the static elements of the representation; what matters is that it behaves as much as possible like the real world object.

OOPs

This idea that a data structure plus its operations form some sort of fundamental entity has given rise to a revolution in programming - one of a number of revolutions going on at the moment! The **Object Oriented Programming** (OOPs) method tries to reduce the whole process of programming to the creation of data structures complete with their associated operations. A data structure complete with its operations is often referred to as an **abstract data type**. I suppose that the ideal that lurks in the mind of the OOPs programmer is that you write a program by defining data objects and then let them get on with working together - just like they do in the real world. For example, if you wanted to simulate a motor car you would define objects for all the parts of the engine, bodywork, suspension etc. and they would all fit together to give you a working motor car. Then you could define a road, city, motorway - it's difficult to see where it all ends! In practice everything doesn't work as powerfully as this ideal suggests and you do have to consider how the objects interact.

Languages are available that are dedicated to implementing the OOPs idea - Smalltalk and Simula for example - but other advanced languages - Ada and Modula-2 - contain features that allow a programmer to adopt the OOPs approach. Essentially all you need to adopt the object oriented approach is some form of information hiding. The C++ language goes further than Ada and Modula-2, but not quite as far as Smalltalk, in its support of Object Oriented programming. Indeed one of the problems with C++ is that it is built as an extension to C and this means that a C programmer can make use of all the nice additional features without really having to adopt the object oriented philosophy. Once you have decided that data objects are the key to building programs then you start to see other desirable properties of the language and programming environment that you are using. For example, most objects that you want to define are very similar to other objects. To avoid starting from scratch each time, object oriented environments provide inheritance rules that allow new objects to be created from old. However many of the object oriented ideas are simply old friends dressed up in new jargon and this can make it difficult to penetrate the approach.

The only requirement a language must posses to allow the object oriented approach to be used, is to provide static local variables that a module can use to store and keep hidden its internal state. Specifically object oriented languages usually provide more, but this is all that is necessary. For example, Pascal and C cannot be used as object oriented languages without the introduction of new commands that **construct,** i.e. bring into existence, objects. Some also supply destructors that deallocate the static storage once the useful life of the object is complete. For example, the approach taken by Turbo Pascal 5.5 is to extend the definition of a record type to include procedures and to allow commands that were originally used to allocate storage for dynamic variables to be used to bring such objects into existence.

To give you some idea of how the object oriented approach works, consider the problem of providing a simple counter. The normal approach to this is to simply use a variable, i say and increment it, i=i+1, and decrement it, i=i-1, as required. A slightly more object oriented approach would be to provide procedures for the operations of increment and decrement i.e. incr(i) and decr(i). The procedures could be used to increment and decrement any counter but there is still nothing to stop the program from using the counter directly and even performing illegal operations such as i=i+7 to 'adjust' its value. The true object oriented method would define a counter object complete with three methods - increment, decrement and accessvalue. The program wouldn't be able to get at the variable used to do the actual counting except by using the methods provided. Clearly the counter variable has to be a static local variable otherwise its value would be lost between each use of the object. In C++ a counter object would be defined as follows

```
CLASS counter
{PRIVATE:
    int:c;
PUBLIC:
    counter() {c=0};
    void increment(){c=c+1};
    void decrement(){c=c-1};
    int access() {RETURN c}
};
```

The PRIVATE keyword declares that c, an integer, is a static local variable. The PUBLIC keyword allows other routines to access the procedures and functions listed below it. The counter method is a constructor. That is, when it is called it allocates storage for the static local variables. The constructor method is distinguished from the others by having the same name as the object, i.e. counter in this case. In addition to creating an object, a C++ constructor can also contain code to initialise the static local variables. In this case it sets the counter to zero. What you might not have realised is that this object definition has to be treated more like a type definition. That is, it isn't an object in itself but a recipe for producing an object. In the jargon this defines an object class and this can be used to create **instances** of the class. Notice that this is just like creating a new data type and then using it to declare variables of this type. For example, if a program needs two counter objects called i and j they could be constructed by using the calls

>counter i;
>counter j;

These calls create instances of the object counter and allocate static local storage for i and j as well as methods for each. Notice that you shouldn't think of this as allocating storage for a variable called i and one called j but as creating complete objects called i and j. After an object has been constructed you can make use of its methods by simply calling the appropriate functions and procedures. Which instance these are to apply to is determined by writing the name of the instance in front of the method's name. For example, a program could increment i by i.increment and increment j by j.increment. Notice that there is no way that the program can get at the counting variable in any other way. If it wants to use the value in the counter then it has to use the function i.access.

Of course, implementing a counter in this way is a small example that doesn't show the full method off to its best advantage but it is compact enough for you to see the essential details of the method.

OOPs is a powerful method and many programmers are definitely committed to using it. Many other programmers are a little worried that all of the progress that has been made in understanding the way that we program is about to be thrown away in a free-for-all defining of objects. At the moment OOPs is at a very early stage in its development and its real contribution to the philosophy of programming is perhaps yet to be made. The major tasks that OOPs programmers have to face is to find ways of making their creations less personal and more maintainable.

OOPs and WIMPs!

There is a strange link between OOPS and WIMP - Windows, Icons, Menus and Pointers - user interfaces. If you have used GEM, Windows or a MAC then you will have come across the idea of using graphics symbols (Icons) to represent familiar everyday objects such as files etc.. Not only are the objects supposed to be familiar but they are supposed to work in the same way. On the MAC you can pick up a file and drag it to the waste bin and drop it in. The waste bin bulges as more files are put into it and eventually it has to be emptied after which the files are permanently deleted. Before emptying it you can retrieve a file by going through the bin. You can see that the waste bin icon is a metaphor for the real world and has all the properties of the real thing that are considered relevant. You can also use a calculator that looks like a calculator, a clock that looks like a clock and so on.. This is the user equivalent of representing external world objects within the machine and it is no accident that the two ideas have their origins in the Xerox Smalltalk project. WIMP interfaces are still developing. The latest ideas are to include simulated people to do jobs for you and the addition of appropriate sound effects. For example, a rustling noise of paper hitting the waste bin when you delete a file and so on. It is almost as if the internal data objects are breaking the surface and becoming the user interface! Both WIMPs and OOPs are part of a common trend towards producing a simulated reality as an operating environment. There are programmers who believe that one day programming will also be just a matter of WIMPs.

key points

- There are a small number of fundamental data types all built from integers and real numbers.

- More complex data types are constructed by applying a structuring method to the fundamental types.

- Most languages provide some static structuring methods but leave the programmer to build the more complex dynamic types.

- A good representation of the real world will share as many of its properties as possible without introducing additional ones.

- The OOPs approach treats the whole problem of programming as constructing appropriate data types and their associated operations.

- The OOPs approach is complementary to the use of WIMP user interfaces and the two represent a common trend.

Chapter Six
Formal programming methods

Now that we have looked at the essential ingredients that make a program, and at some of the deeper principles that are behind program construction, the time has come to look at some of the many formal programming methods that are available. It is important to distinguish at this early stage the difference between a formal **programming method** and a **systems design** method. A programming method aims to formalise, i.e. give a recipe for, how a program is derived from the statement of a problem. This method should try to minimise the need for divine inspiration or creativity. In other words it should be as close to automated programming as possible. Of course no design method achieves this ideal and the best that we can hope for is a method that helps us select appropriate techniques and organise our work in an efficient manner.

A systems design method is more concerned with the design and management of large programming projects. That is, systems design methods take a broader view of the activity of program development. As a result they say far less about the philosophy of program construction and more about project management.

Another term that is often used to refer to the whole gamut of programming methods is **software engineering**. This is a vague term that is best defined as the very opposite of just sitting down and writing a program that happened to pop into your head. In other words it attempts to treat software development as if it was just a branch of engineering. All of the methods described in this book could be listed under this heading.

Commercial methods

One thing that it is worth keeping in mind when you try to learn about any particular programming method is that there is generally a commercial interest. Most programming methods have been developed in traditional data processing departments which spend most of their time working with sequential files, records, databases and mostly in Cobol. This accounts for the bias in most programming methods for dealing with just these topics. So for example, there are very few programming methods that consider problems such as compiler writing, operating system design, AI programs etc.. The programming method's world is firmly DP oriented.

You might think that academic computer scientists would have tried to redress this balance. Well in a sense they have. The ideas of program structure and modular programming described in the previous chapters are academic in their origins and they constitute the programming method usually referred to as **Top Down Modular Structured Programming** or **TDMSP**. Even so, as described in the previous chapters, TDMSP seems more a natural consequence of what a program is, rather than a formal method. However this is precisely what a good programming method should be like - natural and obvious. Otherwise it is simply forcing programming and programs to be something that they are not. It is also worth remembering that there are many programmers who do not consider TDMSP obvious and program in a very different and primitive way - without using subroutines and with an ad hoc structure. For these programmers TDMSP does indeed have the flavour of a formal method!

However after TDMSP the academic world has concentrated on highly abstract methods of program proof and program construction from formal problem descriptions. At the moment these methods are only workable for small scale programs because they involve a great deal of effort. They are also attempts to reduce programming to mathematics and as such they remove much of what makes programming special. Mathematical statements are static but the text of a program is dynamic. An alternative approach to these formal methods, that also attempts to make a program text static, is **declarative programming**. This reduces a program to a statement of relationships between variables which the computer has to maintain. Declarative programming is at the moment a much more practical method as the success of Prolog, a declarative language, proves. Even so at the moment declarative programming occupies specific applications areas such as AI rather than having the broad spread of a general purpose language such as C, Pascal, Ada, BASIC etc..

Another important aspect of many commercial programming methods is that, as well as being designed for a very particular market, they are also marketed! That is there is a profit to be made in teaching a particular method and each method is touted and sold in much the same way as a washing powder. The main difference being that programming methods lend themselves to a glamorisation by mystification process. Hence, in spite of the extensive marketing it can be very difficult to find out exactly what any given programming method consists of. When you add the sometimes elaborate and not particularly descriptive jargon to the already vague steps involved in most methods, it can be difficult to see the trees for the fog! As a result many programmers are under the impression that there is something powerful hidden deep within these methods - there isn't. All programming methods are based on some way of making use of a consideration of the real world data to select appropriate representations and then using these representations to generate the procedures as straightforwardly as possible.

At a more basic level this corresponds to the self evident truth that most programmers know that once you have sorted out the data representation then the program more or less writes itself, with you acting as a willing helper. Some programmers never really seem to come to terms with data and as a result, no matter how much structured programming they learn or apply, their programs are an unnatural mess. The first group of programming methods - **functional decomposition** - all attempted to make use of the data structure to show how the program hierarchy could be developed in a way that suited or meshed with the data structure. A characteristic of these methods is that they all assume that the translation from the real world to the internal data structure is either not necessary because the problem starts from an internal data structure - i.e. a file of records - or they assume that the connection between the two is obvious. The two best know methods in this group are **Jackson Structured Programming (JSP)** and **Data flow design**. These are briefly described in this chapter.

The only real alternative to functional decomposition is **Object Oriented Design** or **OOD**. The only real problem is that at the moment it appears that object oriented design is the same thing as object oriented programming. That is, it seems to be difficult to disentangle the philosophy of object oriented programming from any considerations of how best to go about using the object oriented approach to solve a problem. It may be that in time such methods will be discovered or it may be that object oriented programming is all that is needed.

Data flow design

There are a number of slightly different programming methods that are based upon the observation that in many DP situations the whole operation can be well described by the flow of data from one place to another. For example, in the simplest situation data may be entered, stored on disk and then output unchanged to a printer. This data flow is clearly so trivial that it hardly needs a program to supervise it. In practice data doesn't flow unchanged from one place to another, this just corresponds to storage, instead it is processed or transformed. It is the nature of these transformations, and more importantly how they involve and relate to the different data flows in a real situation, that is important and that allows the program hierarchy to be derived. The ideas of data flow design are usually associated with the names of Yourdon, Constantine, DeMarco, Gane and Sarson.

The first stage in any form of data flow design is to draw a **data flow diagram**. There are many different types of standard symbol used to draw a data flow diagram but most use a circle augmented by a number of logical symbols that place restrictions on the nature of the input or output that the stage accepts or produces. The basic symbols are + to mean either data item may be accepted or produced and * to mean that both data items must be accepted or produced. (These are clearly just OR and AND operators.)

The main feature of a data flow diagram is that it shows the transformations that the data is subjected to without being specific about how the transformations are implemented, or even the exact sequencing of operations. This is an advantage because it allows the programmer to explore

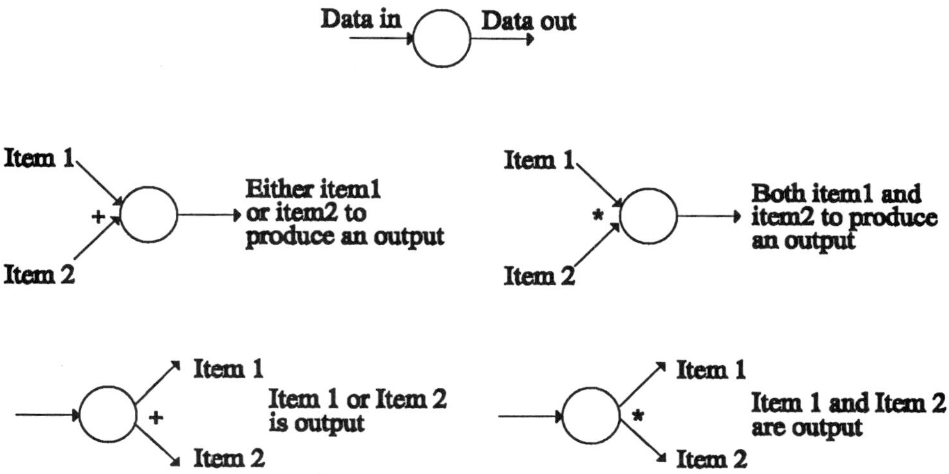
Data in
Data out
Item 1
+
Item 2
Either item1
or item2 to
produce an output
Item 1
*
Item 2
Both item1 and
item2 to produce
an output
Item 1
+
Item 2
Item 1 or Item 2
is output
Item 1
*
Item 2
Item 1 and Item 2
are output

the nature of the entire system before becoming committed to a detailed design. It is also a disadvantage because much of the skill in using the data flow method is in converting the data flow diagram into a program structure. As the data flow diagram does not of itself imply a hierarchy of operations there are usually many program structures derivable from any single data flow diagram. The best that most data flow methods can do is to provide guidelines about how to go about deriving a program structure.

Give a data flow diagram, the first stage is to derive a rough hierarchy of program modules represented by drawing a diagram where each module corresponds to a box complete with a description of what the module does and an indication of the data it receives and the data it outputs. This is generally referred to as a **program structure diagram**. This diagram can then be refined by adding increasing amounts of detail and extending the depth of the hierarchy by repeatedly splitting modules.

The only question that remains is how to derive a program structure diagram from a data flow diagram and this is where the different methods offer alternative approaches. They all however concentrate on the problem of finding a reasonable mapping of the fairly free data flow in the data flow diagram into the more constrained flow of data up and down the hierarchy of modules. To aid this process it helps to identify, at least, four types of module in the hierarchy according to the way data passes through them

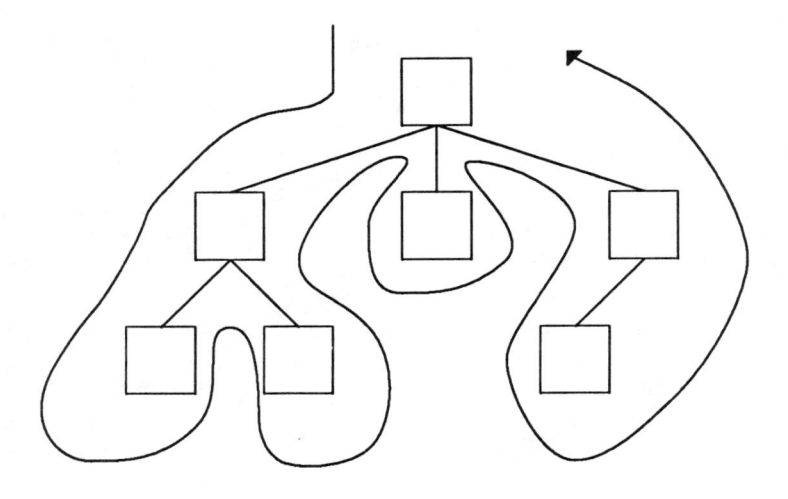

Data flow around a hierarchy of modules

1) Input modules - these accept input from lower level modules and pass it on, possibly modified, to higher level modules.

2) Output modules - these accept input from higher level modules and pass it down, possibly modified, to lower level modules.

3) Transform modules - these accept data from a higher level module and pass it back to that module in a modified form.

4) Coordinating modules - these are responsible for coordinating and managing other modules.

Different data flow methods use different jargon and definitions for these module types. For example, **afferent** for input modules and **efferent** for output modules. Whatever they are called, these modules are the building blocks from which the program structure diagram has to be assembled and the skill in using the data flow method is in identifying these modules within the data flow diagram. There are many guidelines for doing this but essentially it still needs a certain amount of skill. In most programs the sequence of operations is such that input is followed by processing which is then followed by an output phase. As long as the data flow diagram corresponds to this input- process-ouput structure, and most do,

Data flow design

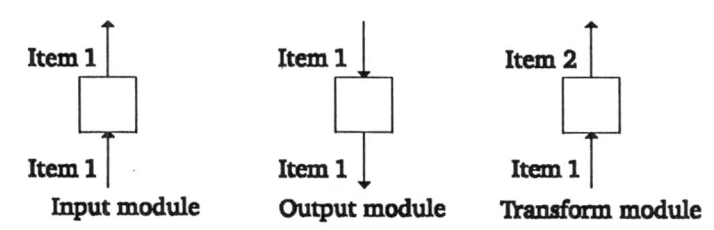

```
     Item 1 ↑              Item 1 ↓            Item 2 ↑
      ┌─┐                   ┌─┐                 ┌─┐
      └─┘                   └─┘                 └─┘
     Item 1 ↑              Item 1 ↓            Item 1 ↑
   Input module          Output module       Transform module
```

then you can convert it into a program structure diagram by identifying the boundaries between input, transform and output stages. Even this can be difficult and so there are a number of guidelines designed to help fix the boundary. For example, if you can find a transformation in the data flow which is sufficiently involved that the input cannot be deduced from the output then this is called a central transform. Once you have identified a **central transformation** you can draw a first level structure diagram with the central transformation as the process section. You can then repeat this procedure, splitting modules to produce modules at lower levels in the hierarchy, until each stage in the data flow is represented on the structure diagram.

The method described above only works as long as the data flow is of the input-process-output type. This is usually called **transformation analysis**. Alternative methods can be used if the data flow corresponds to other overall patterns. For example, if the data flow is such that the process selected depends on the input data then the method is called **transactional analysis**. In this case the program structure takes the form of an input section, a transaction selector and a range of modules that are called by it according to nature of the input data.

As a simple example consider the data flow for the update of a telephone directory. If you do this by the very inefficient method of reading in a new record, appending it to the existing database and then sorting the result the data flow can be represented as

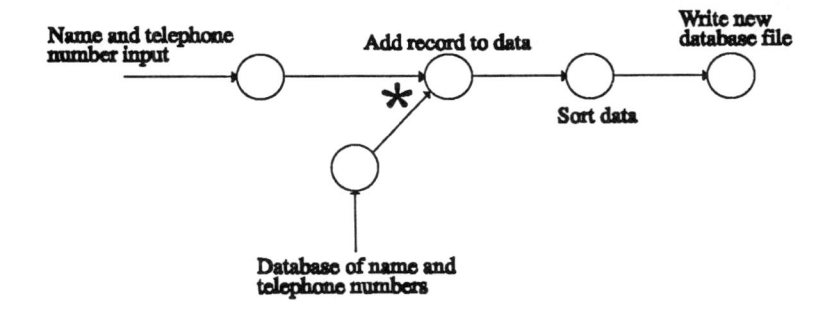

```
Name and telephone        Add record to data       Write new
number input                                       database file
       ────────○──────────────○───────────○──────────○
                              *
                              │
                              ○
                              │
                       Database of name and
                       telephone numbers
                                         Sort data
```

Clearly in this case the central transformation is the sort operation and the first stage structure diagram is simply input, sort and output. After a little more work the finished structure diagram is

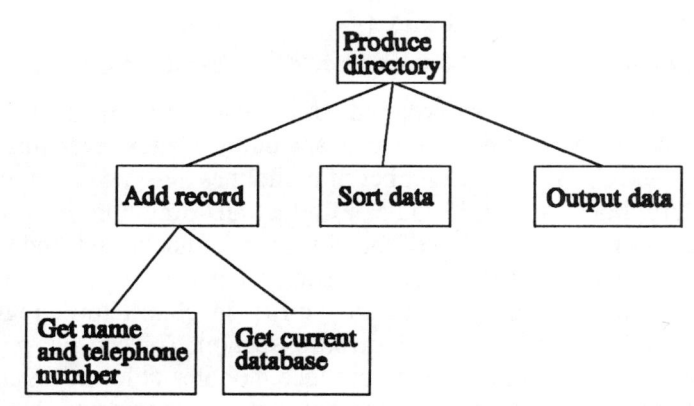

```
                    ┌──────────┐
                    │ Produce  │
                    │ directory│
                    └──────────┘
          ┌──────────────┼──────────────┐
    ┌───────────┐  ┌───────────┐  ┌───────────┐
    │ Add record│  │ Sort data │  │Output data│
    └───────────┘  └───────────┘  └───────────┘
      ┌──────┴──────┐
┌────────────┐ ┌────────────┐
│ Get name   │ │Get current │
│and telephone│ │ database  │
│ number     │ │            │
└────────────┘ └────────────┘
```

Of course in a real problem the data flow diagram would be much larger and more than one structure diagram would be derivable from it.

As well as guidelines for converting data flow diagrams into structure diagrams, most data flow methods include a great many other rules of thumb designed to help the programmer. For example, one often quoted is that a module in a structure diagram should have between two and seven subordinate modules. This is based on psychological research that shows that human short term memory has a span of seven items plus or minus two. This is often referred to as the 'magic number seven plus or minus two' rule from the original title of the paper that presented the result. You can find lots of applications of this rule in computing but they all more or less come down to the 'keep it simple' principle. It is important not to become too enthusiastic about the number seven. In any real situation there are other factors that govern simplicity in addition to the number of items. For example, a module that consists of nothing but read statements is easy to understand even if it is fairly long but throw in few selects and loops of the same length and the average programmer would soon be lost. It is the **perceived complexity** as well as raw number of modules, lines, or anything else that is important.

Data structure methods

The main problem with data flow analysis is that it doesn't take any account of any structure that the data may have. In many situations the actual flow of data is a trivial 'source to sink' with a simple transformation in between. However when you come to construct the program structure the program is more complex because of the structure of the data. There are a number of programming methods that work directly from the structure of the data, the best known being due to Warnier and Jackson. The difference between the two is mainly one of notation although the Jackson method does go rather further in its consideration of how to tackle difficulties that occur. The remainder of this chapter describes Jackson Structured Programming (JSP) as it seems to represent the closest thing we have to a coherent programming method.

JSP

JSP starts from a view of data as something regular that can be described using the programming constructs of sequencing, repetition and selection. For example, if you have a data file composed of groups of records of type T2 and each group always starts with an identifying record of type T1 then you can see that this is a sequence with repetition. Indeed it is composed of two repeats - the repetition of the group (T1, any number of T2s) and the repetition of the T2s. To see this more clearly consider a program that would generate such a file

```
        DO UNTIL file end
           WRITE T1
           DO UNTIL group end
              WRITE T2
           LOOP
        LOOP
```

In JSP it is usual to draw the structure of the data using a **structure diagram**. This is composed of boxes arranged in a hierarchy showing the various sub components of the data. If A is composed of a sequence of parts, say B C D then this would be shown as

```
    ┌───┐
    │ A │
    └─┬─┘
  ┌───┼───┐
┌─┴─┐┌┴┐┌─┴─┐
│ B ││C││ D │
└───┘└─┘└───┘
```

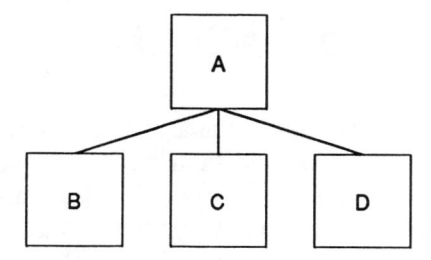

If one of the parts can be repeated any number of times (including zero) then it is drawn with an asterisk in the top right hand corner. For example,

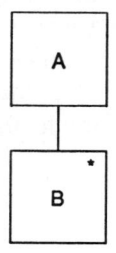

```
┌───┐
│ A │
└─┬─┘
┌─┴─┐*
│ B │
└───┘
```

means that A is made up of a sequence of repeated Bs. You can show selection between alternatives by drawing a small circle in the top right hand corner. For example

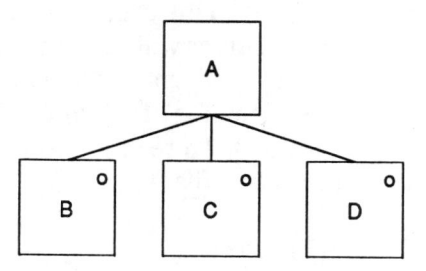

```
     ┌───┐
     │ A │
     └─┬─┘
  ┌────┼────┐
┌─┴─┐°┌┴┐°┌─┴─┐°
│ B │ │C│ │ D │
└───┘ └─┘ └───┘
```

means that A is either a B, a C or a D.

Using these conventions the structure diagram for the data file described earlier is

```
        ┌──────┐
        │ File │
        └───┬──┘
            │
        ┌───┴──┐ *
        │Record│
        │group │
        └───┬──┘
       ┌────┴────┐
   ┌───┴──┐  ┌───┴──┐
   │  T1  │  │ Sub  │
   │      │  │group │
   └──────┘  └───┬──┘
                 │
             ┌───┴──┐ *
             │  T2  │
             └──────┘
```

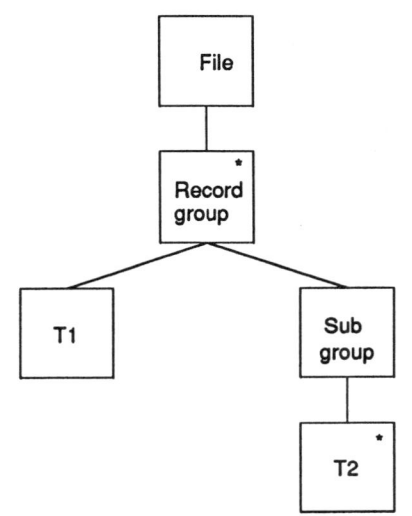

Why sequential files?

As is the case with most programming methods, JSP was developed in a mainly Cobol/mainframe environment where a lot of the problems were concerned with processing sequential files. This has resulted in many a programmer deciding that JSP was only good for such problems - this isn't the case. The main characteristic of a sequential file is that the program has access to the data in a particular order. The data can be accumulated in a record buffer to allow for a certain amount of 'direct access' but even this forces the program to work with sequential chunks of data. Most input and output data is sequential, even if it has nothing to do with a file. For example, someone typing on a keyboard generates characters sequentially. These characters usually have a regular pattern that can be described using a structure diagram and so JSP can be used. In the same way the output of a program to screen or printer is a sequence of characters that can be described by a structure diagram, as is a sequence of readings from almost any peripheral device, etc.. In short the sequential file is the most common form of data to be found in computing.

Structure diagrams to programs

The basic idea behind JSP is easy enough to express but it can be slightly more tricky to apply in practice. If you have a structure diagram corresponding to the data that a program is going to process, then the structure of the program can be derived from it. This doesn't seem too unreasonable if you think back to the file of records example given earlier. The structure of the data corresponds to a pair of nested repetitions and this is indeed the structure of the program needed to generate such a file. The dogma of JSP says that not only is this true in this case, but for any program that processes the same data. The reasoning is that the data structure diagram shows the order in which the program will meet the data and so the program needs a corresponding section to deal with each part of the data. For example, a program that counted the number of T2 records in the data file would have the structure

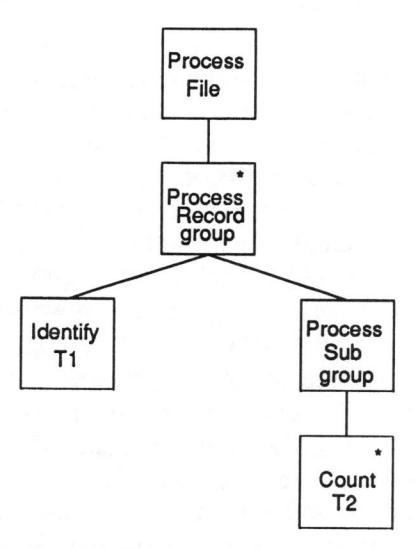

```
            ┌──────────┐
            │ Process  │
            │  File    │
            └────┬─────┘
                 │
            ┌────┴─────┐ *
            │ Process  │
            │ Record   │
            │  group   │
            └────┬─────┘
         ┌───────┴───────┐
    ┌────┴───┐      ┌────┴────┐
    │Identify│      │ Process │
    │   T1   │      │   Sub   │
    │        │      │  group  │
    └────────┘      └────┬────┘
                         │
                    ┌────┴────┐ *
                    │  Count  │
                    │   T2    │
                    └─────────┘
```

You should be able to see that this corresponds to the data structure apart from the change in the labels. Of course in practice you will need to elaborate this structure to include details such as initialising and updating a counter, ending conditions for the loops etc., but even if you add boxes for such things the overall structure will remain the same.

Structure clashes

If you are using JSP the first thing that you do is to write down a structure diagram for the data that your program is working with. Then you convert this into a diagram of your program and then translate the diagram into the final code or into a high level **pseudo code**. (A pseudo code is simply an invented computer language that can be mixed with English descriptions of what happens.)

The only trouble with this neat method is that there are usually a number of data structures involved in a program. In most cases there are at least two - an input data structure and an output data structure. JSP says that a successful program should reflect the structure of all of the data not just one particular portion of it. For example, if you are reading in a square matrix line by line and printing it out line by line then it is easy to see that the input and output data structures are identical and combining them is no problem.

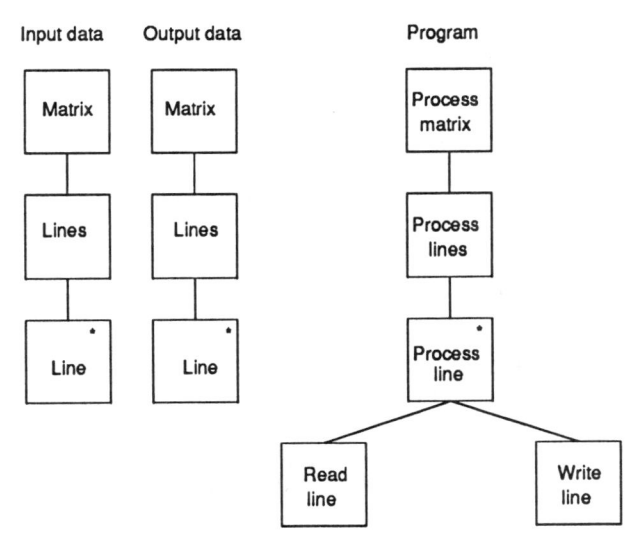

```
Input data      Output data              Program

  Matrix          Matrix               Process
                                       matrix
    |               |                     |
  Lines           Lines                Process
                                       lines
    |               |                     |
  Line            Line                 Process
                                       line
                                       /      \
                                   Read       Write
                                   line       line
```

However in a real case the way in which the data structures should be combined can be a problem. There are even cases where the data structures are so different that they cannot be combined without gross distortion of one or more of them. This situation is called a **structure clash** and when it happens a program is difficult to write. For example, if you need a program that will read a matrix by row and print it by column then you cannot merge the two data structures.

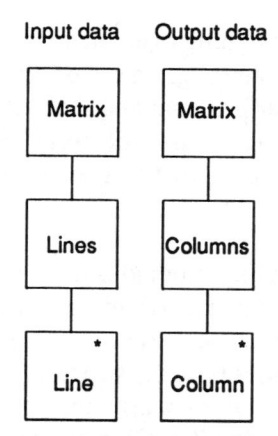

```
        Input data     Output data

         ┌──────┐       ┌───────┐
         │Matrix│       │Matrix │
         └──┬───┘       └───┬───┘
            │               │
         ┌──┴───┐       ┌───┴───┐
         │Lines │       │Columns│
         └──┬───┘       └───┬───┘
            │ *             │ *
         ┌──┴───┐       ┌───┴───┐
         │ Line │       │Column │
         └──────┘       └───────┘
```

The solution that any most programmers would opt for is to use some sort of intermediate storage - either a simple file that could be sorted from row to column order or direct access storage. In either case the single program is broken down into two programs that communicate via the intermediate storage.

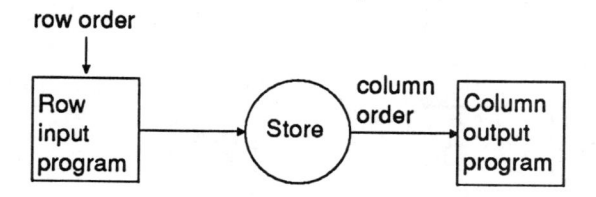

```
   row order                        column
      │                              order
      ▼
  ┌───────┐                        ┌────────┐
  │ Row   │          ╱───╲         │ Column │
  │ input │────────▶│Store│───────▶│ output │
  │program│          ╲───╱         │program │
  └───────┘                        └────────┘
```

This is the standard JSP way of dealing with a structure clash. It recognises the fact that a single program cannot have two structures at the same time but using intermediate storage is often inefficient. In practice structure clashes can be a great deal more complex than this simple example and it can even be difficult to detect when the situation has arisen!

JSP and regular expressions

There is a very strong connection between JSP and the mathematics of syntax analysis. The basic components of a structure diagram are in fact identical to the grammar of regular expressions. This isn't really very surprising as both are concerned with describing the regularities found in data.

A regular expression is one that is formed using repetition and selection. Roughly speaking regular expressions are defined by giving a template that describes their regularities. The symbol for repetition is * and any character followed by * can be repeated any number of times. The symbol for selection is l and it is used to separate alternative forms. For example, A* defines data that consists of strings of any number of A's. The template A*BA* defines data that consists of strings of the form B, AB, ABA, AAB, ABAAA etc. in other words any number of As followed by a B followed by any number of As. Notice that in this context any number of As includes none at all. The template A*lB* defines strings that consist of any number of As or any number of Bs. A more complicated pattern is (AB)* which give rise to strings like AB, ABAB etc..

You should be able to see that a regular expression to describe the format of the data file composed of records of type T1 and T2 used earlier in this chapter is simply T1 T2*. In the same way any structure diagram has its associated regular expression. At this point you may think that this association is interesting but nothing more. However there is a well developed theory that shows how to automatically construct a program that will recognise a regular expression. That is, when given a regular expression supposed to be an example of the template, the program will decide if this is so.

This notion of augmenting the program that recognises a regular expression with actions and further conditions such as the number of T2 records is very similar to the method of augmenting more advanced recognisers to produce ATNs (Augmented Transition Networks) used to process natural language.

Seen in this light it looks as though JSP is just another way of writing the traditional theory of grammars, but even if you discount some of the additional aspects of JSP, such as inversion and backtracking (see later), it still goes one stage further. JSP maintains that the program is constructed from a consideration of the structure of the input data and the output data - that is two regular expressions. Clearly what we have to do is construct a program that can recognise the regular expression that is the input data while producing a corresponding regular expression that is the output data. If the two types of data have enough in common, i.e. if one is a subset of the other, then this indeed will be possible but if they don't then the two regular grammars will give rise to two very different programs. In other words the two types of regular expressions cannot be recognised by a single machine. This situation corresponds to what is known in JSP as a structure clash.

What this means is that JSP does have a sound theoretical basis and a whole range of techniques available to it that are normally ignored. However this still doesn't mean that it can be reduced to simple syntax analysis. For example, the structure diagram does convey more information to most programmers than a corresponding regular expression. Also it is probably better to use the structure diagrams as an aid in producing a program than allowing an automatic method to generate a recognition program that then has to be modified to produce the desired results. In other words JSP allows the programmer to combine in a flexible and natural manner semantic and syntactic information concerning the program and its data structures.

Program inversion

JSP offers a solution to the inefficiency of using an intermediate file as a communications medium between programs that are the result of a structure clash. It is known as **program inversion**. The basic idea is that one of the programs can be converted into a subroutine to be called by the other. The rules for converting the program are straightforward. If you are converting the second program into a subroutine of the first then each READ statement in the first becomes a call to the second and each WRITE in the second becomes a return. The main difference between a subroutine that arises from inversion and an ordinary subroutine is that it has to remember where it has got to between calls. This is most easily done by the use of static state variables.

All of this sounds either academic or trite depending on your point of view until you have seen an example. A common structure clash is caused by the use of fixed size disk sectors to store records. All of the read/write operations on the file are performed in terms of sectors of one size but the program wants to process records of another size. In this case we have an example of a **boundary clash** - the two data streams are the same but divided up in different and mildly incompatible ways.

The non-inverted solution would be to write one program that read sectors and wrote records to an intermediate file and a second program that read records. This is obviously inefficient and may not even be possible given the hardware constants. The inverted solution is to write the first program as a subroutine of the second. Each time the second program wanted to read a record it would call the first, which would simply read sectors until it had a complete record and then would return this as a result. Suppose that each record was 1.5 sectors then the first time that the inverted subroutine was called it would have to read 2 sectors from disk and to return the data in the first 1.5 to the calling program. The second time that the inverted subroutine was called it would have to remember the .5 of a sector still in its buffers and only read an additional 1 sector before returning a new complete record. It is clear that the inverted subroutine has to keep track of its internal state. In this case all that is necessary is a state variable, S say, that is set to 1 if there is part of a sector already in the buffer. In other cases you might need to record more than just two possible states.

The description above makes it sound as though JSP is of little help in solving structure clashes by programming inversion because of the need to construct the inverted subroutine by hand. This isn't the case. The purpose of the example was to explain what program inversion is and how it differs from a standard subroutine by showing its inner detail. The JSP method recommends that a programmer resolves structure clashes by writing two simple programs that communicate via intermediate storage and then use a more or less automatic process to invert one of them. Program inversion is viewed as a detail of implementation not a design method.

Read ahead and backtracking

If you build your program on the basis of the data structures it has to process, you will eventually come across the problem of not being able to decide what to do until you have read a quite a lot of the data. JSP deals with this problem by suggesting that programs can read ahead in the data stream. Many approaches to programming take the view that every program should only read or write data in one place. This is because it is thought to be difficult to keep track of where you are in a data stream if different parts of your program can read data in. Of course if you are using JSP then this is rubbish because you always know where you are in the data stream by where you are in the program - the program structure mimics the data structure. It is suggested that a read should be executed before entering the part of the program that processes the data. For example, in the case of the file of T1 and T2 records described earlier, the first READ would be carried out in the process file module and, after dealing with a T1 record, another READ would be carried out before moving on to the T2 record processing module. In this way each part of the program would be entered with the data that it needed to read and would read the data needed for the next stage before finishing.

Read ahead often allows you to decide which stage of processing should be used next, but this is not always the case. Very often it is not possible to decide what should happen next until you have processed the data. If there are two or more alternative types of processing how can you choose which one should be carried out? The answer is that you can't. Instead JSP tells us to design a program that initially processes the data based on the most likely type of data and, if it turns out that the guess was wrong, all we have to do is **backtrack** to the dividing of the ways within the program and continue with the correct procedure. JSP includes a definition of how to organise backtracking efficiently but it's the basic idea of using backtracking as a programming structure that is the innovation. For example, you can use it to avoid many of the complex situations that often require exception or error handling. If you are trying to work out something complicated and halfway through the calculation it turns out that you cannot complete the task, because the data values are unsuitable in some way, then you would normally have to give up with a system or internal error or use something sophisticated like exception handling. If instead you use backtracking then you can effectively place a test at the start of the calculation something like

IF calculation possible THEN calculate result ELSE deal with problem

Of course this IF statement is silly because you cannot know if the calculation is possible until you have tried to calculate the result. However backtracking allows you to behave as if this was known all the time. What happens in practice is that the calculate result module would be called and if it couldn't complete and exit normally then the whole program would backtrack to the IF statement and the ELSE part would be carried out! A simple bending of time to suit the program's logic seems perfectly reasonable.

Using JSP

JSP is an interesting programming technique because it makes the data structures central to the creation of a program but it isn't a complete theory. For one thing it starts at the point when the data is more or less in computer form. The regularity in the data structures which JSP exploits is more or less imposed on the real world objects at a stage that JSP doesn't consider. For example, someone must have decided to make a file composed of type T1 and T2 records with a particular internal format but in the data structure given earlier this decision was ignored. If you are in the position that either the real world data has an obvious internal representation or someone else has decided on that representation then JSP does start from the beginning of the process.

A second problem with JSP, and with all current programming methods, is that it still isn't tightly controlled enough to stop a poor programmer making a mess of it. There is generally more than one way of drawing a structure diagram. Which one a programmer actually draws or is aware of will affect their solution. In the process of combining separate data structures into a single program structure there is scope for choice and hence bad choices.

However perhaps the biggest shortcoming of JSP is that it takes into account the structure of the input data and the structure of the output data but it takes far less notice of the process that is to connect them. Problems often arise where the data structures are virtually structureless but the operations to be implemented are complex.

When JSP works without the need for the programmer to make choices it is more or less identical to program construction by syntax analysis. The structure diagram corresponds to a grammar for the data and the program structure is a parser for that grammar. Once you get beyond this simple situation then JSP is no more than a framework that helps you to think about your program in simple and data related ways.

Diagrams and CASE

Many books on programming methods emphasise the idea of graphical representation right from the start. The most usual form of program related diagram is the **flow chart** - a diagram of the flow of control that includes descriptions of the actions performed at each step. Flow charts that contain a high degree of detail are semantically equivalent to the program they represent. That is you could invent a way of compiling them into a working program - they are a programming language. In this sense constructing a flow chart is little different from writing the program in the language of your choice. The best that can be said for the flow chart is that it once kept programmers from using valuable machine time by forcing them to write their program twice - once as a flow chart and once in the language that the machine offered.

Diagrams and CASE   135

The inadequacy of the flow chart doesn't force the conclusion that all graphical methods are inadequate. Indeed one of the most powerful aspects of both the data flow and the JSP method are the diagrams that they both insist that you draw. In the case of the data flow diagram all data files, inputs and outputs are shown along with some information about how they relate. A JSP data structure diagram similarly documents the structure of the data and a program structure diagram is a map of the overall layout of the program. You should be able to see that there are many complementary aspects of data flow and JSP and there is no reason not to make use of their diagramming methods even if you do not subscribe to the rest of their philosophy.

It is strange to think that programmers have only just recently thought to make use of the computer itself in their design task. **Computer Aided Software Engineering**, or **CASE**, programs are designed to help the programmer make use of many of the diagramming and other documentation tools and management techniques that the use of a modern programming method demands. A typical CASE tool or workbench will provide a diagramming facility that allows a variety of types of diagram to be constructed. It may even offer checks of consistency and goodness of the diagrams and maintain a central dictionary of names and types. In addition, project management software is also included to enable the programmer or program manager to keep track of what stage the project has reached. Some even include debugging facilities although most of these have been around a lot longer than the idea of CASE. Of course the quality and usability of different CASE tools varies a lot and it is interesting to examine the type of product that programmers create for their own consumption. If car makers produced a car for their own use then it would be luxurious, powerful, technically advanced - in short the best possible. After seeing some CASE tools I have a suspicion that many programmers in the same situation would build the equivalent of a Model T Ford.

CASE is often represented as the way of improving programmer productivity and program quality. This is only true if the programmers using CASE tools know, understand and practice the ideas that they are intended to support. Using a CASE tool isn't a programming method.

Object Oriented Design

The basic ideas of object oriented programming have already been introduced in earlier chapters. At one level object oriented programming is nothing more than a programming technique that can be used to realise a conventional design more reliably. For example, you could use data flow or JSP and then implement the result using objects rather than traditional modules. However it is also possible to see the object oriented approach as being a complete philosophy of how a program should be designed as well as implemented.

Object oriented programming has a simple objective - to create program units that hide all details of their implementation and behave and interact with other modules in ways that mimic the real world objects that they represent. In other words, it is a simulation-based approach to programming. Object oriented design has to at least give some guidelines on how these modules or objects should be identified in the real world and how they should be used to build a program. There are a number of object oriented design methods, for example Hierarchical Object Oriented Design or HOOD but at the moment these are no more than design aids or blends of existing none object oriented design methods.

In most object oriented examples the real world objects are clearly defined and the only problem is the exact details of their implementation - this hardly constitutes a design method and one is hardly needed. For example, if you were implementing a home temperature control program then obvious objects are thermometers, heaters, rooms etc.. This is typical of the examples used to introduce OOPs because they are mostly taken from **real time** or **embedded** programming environments where the simulation metaphor takes on another degree of reality. That is, instead of just pretending that an object is a heater with a controllable level of heat output the heater object actually controls the heat output of a real heater! You can see that reality and simulation are blended in a way that really does give the object oriented approach a natural advantage.

At the moment full object oriented environments such as Smalltalk, are not efficient enough to allow real time programs to be implemented using them. In this case you can either use the object oriented method as a design and then implement it using a procedural language such as Ada or you

Object Oriented Design 137

can use more efficient object oriented languages such as C++ or an object oriented Pascal such as Turbo Pascal 5.5 or Quick Pascal.

However in more complex situations the objects are not so clear cut. For example, when defining a database there can be considerably difficulty in identifying what record objects should be defined. Indeed there are a number of design methods specifically for database that assume particular models - **entity relationship**, **relational** and **network** models. These can be thought of as highly specialised object oriented design methods that attempt to find good representations for record structured data. However the method used in the entity relation model is capable of generalisation.

The first step is to derive entity sets that consist of groups of similar objects. For example, if you are writing a program that keeps a track of bank accounts then possible entity sets are (customers) and (accounts). These entity sets are clearly candidates for implementation as objects. The next stage is to define the attributes which each entity possesses. For example, a customer would have a name, a customer number etc.. These attributes are equally clearly the internal data that defines an object.

Finally the relationships between the entities are defined. In the database example these relationships are static. For example a customer object will be associated or related to an account object. However there is no reason why these relationships shouldn't include a consideration of interactions between objects. So a customer may deposit an amount of money in an account that they own, a person may withdraw an amount from an account by presenting a cheque etc.. These dynamic relationships are nothing more than definitions of the methods to be associated with each object.

You may be wondering whatever happened to the program hierarchy described in Chapter Four. The current view that we have of object oriented programming is that there is just one level - the objects and their interactions. In fact object oriented programming is just as hierarchical as any technique of programming. Indeed an important feature of most object oriented programming languages is that they provide both a top down and a bottom up hierarchy.

The familiar top down hierarchy is represented in two ways - as the functions and procedures which constitute an object's methods and as the breaking down of a single large object into a number of sub-objects. The implementation of an object's methods as separate procedures clearly represents an application of modular programming, however there is nothing to say that an object should show a high degree of cohesion. For example, if an object represents different parts of a machine then it makes sense to implement the subcomponents as distinct objects. This is clearly another application of the top down approach. A motor car object is composed of a mechanics object and a body object. A mechanics object is composed of an engine object, gearbox object, clutch object and so on.

As well as an object being built from a number of sub-objects, it is also possible that an object may be regarded as specialisation of an existing object type. For example, if you have a definition of a vehicle object then perhaps a car object could be defined by slight modification and augmentation of the more general vehicle type. This is supported in nearly all object oriented languages as **inheritance**. A derived object type inherits all of the methods of its parent type and it can also define new methods and redefine inherited methods. As a more realistic example, you could define a stack object as a sub-class of a general list object and only have to define a push method as adding an item to the front of the list and a pop method as removing an item from the front of the list. As adding items to the list are methods inherited by the stack object from the list object this should be easy.

A set of derived objects form an inheritance hierarchy that can be given additional properties to make it even more powerful. For example, some object oriented languages support **multiple inheritance** where methods are inherited from more than one object class. This allows joint objects that are mixtures of existing objects to be created. **Polymorphism** is a technique whereby the appropriate method is selected by searching the inheritance hierarchy etc..

One version of the object oriented philosophy states that the only hierarchical principle to be used in object oriented design is inheritance. That is, the only program construction method allowed is the customisation and reuse of a wide range of baseline object types. It is important that this apparently radical approach is seen for what it is - a bottom up design method. The base line objects represent a module library from which a program can be pieced together. The difference is of course that the modules, i.e. the base line objects, represent the most general example of an object rather the most specific, as is the case in a traditional bottom up design. At the moment the situation is unclear.

Object oriented languages such as Smalltalk provide a large collection of long established base types that makes this approach possible but some programmers don't like it because of the need to know and use so many supplied objects. This has always been an objection to bottom up design, and programming environments such as Smalltalk are attempting to overcome it by providing advanced editing tools such as browsers that allow a programmer to inspect what is available.

At the other extreme, object oriented languages such as C++ provide very few, if any, base line objects and expect programmers to create their own objects from scratch using standard methods, and if inheritance comes in handy so be it. This difference in philosophy is almost accidental but it provides two distinct approaches to object oriented design and may in time provide us with a more complete methodology than either could alone.

key points

- There are two main types of programming method functional decomposition and object oriented design.

- The two main functional programming methods are based on data flow and data structure.

- The data flow method gives guidelines for converting a data flow diagram to a program structure diagram.

- The best known data structure method is JSP and this aims to convert a data structure diagram into a program structure diagram.

- JSP claims that the program structure can be derived by considering both the input and output data structures.

- JSP also defines such useful ideas as structure clash, inversion and backtracking.

- Object oriented design identifies the natural objects and their interactions present in the real world and translates these to objects and methods within the program.

- Object oriented programming encourages the use of a bottom up hierarchy as well as a top down hierarchy.

Chapter Seven
Recursion

It is a well known fact that any program can be written using nothing but sequence, selection and iteration. In this sense these three forms of control are fundamental. However there is a fourth possibility - **recursion**. You can show that anything that can be done using recursion can be achieved without it and in this sense it isn't as fundamental but then anything that you can do with a FOR loop can be done with a combination of IF and GOTO statements. Perhaps what is important is not fundamental status but whether or not recursion corresponds to something else that is natural in programming.

Hard recursion

There are programmers who seem to be born to 'recurse' but the great majority treat it as a strange and even legendary beast that others, mainly in advanced text books, use to solve even stranger problems. This isn't in the least bit unreasonable. All of the traditional programming methods more or less ignore recursion, many programming languages don't support it, and how many people are introduced to recursion early in their programming career? For these reasons many programmers fail to place it in the grand scheme of things even after studying it for some time. They find it difficult to think in terms of recursion and even when they do it still makes them uneasy. I never feel 100% confidence in any program that uses recursion, even if it has been in use for some time without error. Indeed the longer I leave it the more I am sure that I don't understand how

142 Recursion   Chapter Seven

the program works. I'm not alone in this unease as any attempt to find recursion in the index of any book on programming methods or software engineering will prove. If you find it at all then the reference will generally be to a single page either dismissing it or elevating it to the status of an advanced method.

This sounds like a good set of reasons for avoiding recursion but there are times, and more particularly problems, that cry out for recursion. In these cases it is often difficult even to describe informally a solution without using recursion. I suppose you could say that recursion isn't often necessary but when it is nothing else will do the job quite as well.

Recursion is an alternative and more powerful form of repetition. By more powerful I mean that it can express ideas that take more effort to express using **iteration**. This relationship between recursion and iteration is symmetrical in that you can also show that anything that you can do using iteration can be achieved using recursion. In other words recursion is the only sort of repetition that you need to write any program. This has resulted in some advanced languages, e.g. Prolog, offering nothing but recursion as a way of repeating blocks of code. There are also languages, Logo for example, that while allowing normal iteration press the idea of recursion as a form of iteration right from the start.

Self reference

The basic mechanism of recursion is **self reference**. There is the apocryphal entry in a dictionary of computer terms that reads "Recursion see recursion" and this is an accurate, if not adequate, definition! There are two frightening aspects of self reference. The first is the potential **infinity** in circling around the meaning. You can almost imagine reading "Recursion see recursion" forever, but programmers are used to dealing with infinite, or at least potentially infinite, loops so this should minimise this fear. The second is the potential for paradox. For example, try reading this sentence and judge it true or false a few times

THIS SENTENCE IS FALSE

The paradox is clearly that if the sentence is true then the declaration of falsehood is wrong so it is false in which case the declaration is true and so on... You should be able to see that this logical paradox is nothing but a flip flop statement equivalent to

        IF A=TRUE THEN A=FALSE ELSE A=TRUE

This is clear to any programmer but logicians have worried out it for many years because logic lacks that essential ingredient - time. In programming such paradoxes are no problem. Indeed they are almost a part of making recursion work.

The infinite recursion

The fundamental loop, where it all begins you might say, is the simple infinite loop

        List :   instruction 1
                  instruction 2
                  . . .
                GOTO List

or in a more modern dialect without labels

        DO
           instruction 1
           instruction 2
           . . .
        LOOP

both of which repeat the list of instructions forever. The same infinite repetition can be achieved without the paraphernalia of loops by using self reference. If we give the name List to the list of instructions and include the command CALL list then it will again repeat for ever -

        List :   instruction 1
                  instruction 2
                  . . .
                CALL List

This IS recursion even if it looks like a simple infinite loop. So what exactly is the difference? The answer is that the force of the CALL List as opposed to the GOTO List instruction is quite different. When you say GOTO List all that happens is that you change the position from which you or the computer are reading the current instruction. However when you say CALL List and mean it recursively it is assumed that a whole new copy of the list of instructions is produced and you start reading it from the top.

This may seem to be a small and insignificant difference, but it is crucial as we shall see. In Chapter Two it was suggested that the characteristic shape of a loop is a circle - looping is clearly going round and round the same set of instructions over and over again. If the characteristic shape of a loop is a circle then the characteristic shape of recursion is a spiral! The reason for this is that as a new copy of the list of instructions is brought into existence with each recursive call. The result can be thought of as

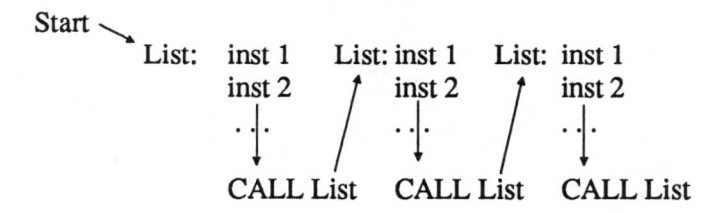

```
Start
     ↘
      List:  inst 1      List: inst 1      List: inst 1
             inst 2            inst 2            inst 2
              ·|·        ↗      ·|·       ↗       ·|·
               ↓        /        ↓       /         ↓
            CALL List      CALL List        CALL List
```

and with a little imagination you should be able to see this as a sort of spiral starting a new turn with each new copy of the program. So infinite recursion corresponds to moving down an infinite spiral of control.

Reactivation

Most programmers can cope with the idea of recursion thus far. It is only when you allow the old copies of the instructions to become reactivated that recursion become tricky. For example if each list of instructions is treated as a normal subroutine or procedure then what happens if a procedure ends? The answer is that control is returned to the copy of the procedure just before the one that is ending. Once you can reactivate an old copy of the instructions you have the power to construct limited repeats rather than just infinite loops. For example, the recursive equivalent of the conditional loop

    List: PRINT "HELLO"
    i=i+1
    IF i=5 THEN EXIT LOOP
    GOTO List

is

    List: PRINT "HELLO"
    i=i+1
    IF i=5 THEN RETURN
    CALL List

The recursive version looks very similar to the iterative version but this hides some subtle differences that can trap the unwary. Notice that each CALL to List brings into existence a completely new copy of the routine including all its variables. So the first time that List is obeyed it prints HELLO and then calls a new copy of itself into existence. The situation at this point is

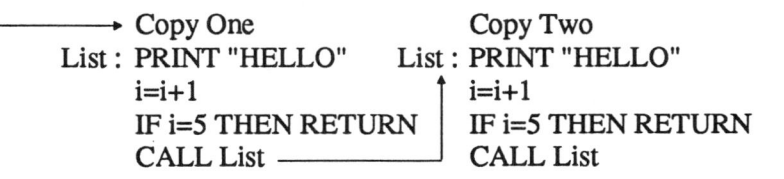

```
─────────► Copy One              Copy Two
    List : PRINT "HELLO"    List : PRINT "HELLO"
           i=i+1         ▲         i=i+1
           IF i=5 THEN RETURN      IF i=5 THEN RETURN
           CALL List ──────────┘   CALL List
```

The question is what is the value in the variable i? If you assume that i started out at zero (an admittedly mucky thing to do as it isn't explicitly initialised), then has one added to it making it one, then in Copy Two of the procedure it has one more added to it making two and so on.. Wrong! The second copy of the procedure is completely new and that includes the variable i. The variable i in the second and subsequent copies of the procedure is local to each copy and has nothing to do with variables in earlier copies.

Clearly if we are going to make recursion into something useful we have to allow some way for the different copies of the procedures to communicate with one another. The solution is, of course to use parameters. A parameter can be used to pass a value into a procedure and a result back out again. Using parameters the correct version of the recursive HELLO program is

```
SUB List(i)
   PRINT "HELLO"
   i=i+1
   IF i=5 THEN RETURN
   CALL List(i)
```

and the whole thing is started off with the call CALL List(0) which initialises i to 0. This version does count the number of HELLOs printed. The first copy of the procedure adds one to its local version of the variable i and then calls List(i) again. This second copy has its local version of i initialised to 1 and so it passes a value of 2 to the next copy of the procedure and so on. Finally a copy of the procedure comes into existence for which i has a value equal to 5 and so the return is executed. Where does this take control back to? The answer is to the statement following the call in the previous copy of the procedure, i.e.

```
Copy Four (i=4)           Copy Five  (i=5)
SUB List(i)               SUB List(i)
PRINT "HELLO"             PRINT "HELLO"
i=i+1                     i=i+1
IF i=5 THEN RETURN        IF i=5 THEN RETURN
CALL List(i) ———————/     CALL List(i)
? ←
```

You can see the problem. As there is no instruction following the CALL nothing happens. This illustrates that you have remember that the statements that you write AFTER a recursive call will be executed when the procedure is reactivated. In this case you could end the procedure with a simple return which would have the effect of 'unwinding' the spiral of recursive calls to take us all the way back to the first copy and then the main program. Notice that for a recursive spiral to come to an end there has to be a conditional exit point before the recursive call itself. This starts the unwinding but from then on the exit point from all the other reactivated copies will be AFTER the recursive call. This means that the last activation of the routine behaves differently from all the others and often has to be treated with care. There is a way of writing the routine to make the last activation behave in the same way to the others. Instead of writing

>SUB List(i)
> PRINT "HELLO"
> i=i+1
>IF i=5 THEN RETURN
> CALL List(i)
>RETURN

where the recursive call is unconditional and the exit conditional, it is easy to see that this can be changed to

>SUB List(i)
> PRINT "HELLO"
> i=i+1
>IF i<5 THEN CALL list(i)
>RETURN

where the recursive call is conditional and the exit unconditional. In this case the final activation behaves in the same way as all the others. That is the instructions that follow the conditional recursive call are obeyed on the way back up the recursive spiral. Many programmers find the second version more difficult to understand but it is easier in the long run.

Value v reference parameters

There is an important difference between recursive calls that use parameters that can pass data into a procedure and those that use parameters that pass data into and out of a procedure. For example, an interesting exercise is to add some statements following the recursive call to print the value of i in the recursive spiral. In other words

>SUB List(i)
> PRINT "HELLO"
> i=i+1
> IF i<5 THEN CALL List(i)
> PRINT i
>RETURN

What does each copy of the procedure print following CALL List(0)? The answer to this question depends on the type of parameter that i is. If i is a value or input parameter then any changes made during the recursive call are not passed back to the calling routine. In other words, the local copy of i passes its value to the next copy of i but any changes to the value aren't passed back. In this form i is a pure input parameter and you can work out what a copy of the routine will print by looking at what value was passed in and what the routine does to that value - you don't have to worry about what any other copy of the routine does to i. You should be able to see that in this case each copy of the routine would print one more than the value passed to it - that is copy 1 prints 1, copy 2 prints 2 and so on. What you might have missed is the order that the numbers are printed. As the recursive sequence unwinds copy 5 prints 5, copy 4 prints 4, copy 3 prints 3, and so on. That is, you see 5,4,3,2,1 printed not, 1,2,3,4,5 as you might expect by the order of activation of the procedures. If you change the routine to

>SUB List(i)
> i=i+1
> PRINT i
> IF i<5 THEN CALL List(i)
> PRINT i
>RETURN

Then you will see 1,2,3,4,5 as the recursion activates each copy of the routine and then 5,4,3,2,1 as they are reactivated on the unwind.

A completely different unwinding behaviour emerges if the parameters passed during the recursive call are passed by reference, i.e. if input/output parameters are used, rather than by value. In this case any changes made by a called routine to the parameter are passed back to the variable in the calling routine. In other words, the parameters are both input and output parameters. You might like to ask yourself what the latest version of the routine would print on the way down and up the recursive spiral. The answer is that nothing changes on the way down i.e. you see 1,2,3,4,5 printed, but on the way back copy 5 of the routine passes the value 5 back to routine 4, which passes 5 back to routine 3 and so on. Thus the answer is 1,2,3,4,5,5,5,5,5,5 a very different behaviour indeed. Although this version of the routine looks less useful it is in fact the more practically useful type of recursion. The reason for this is that it allows the final activation of the routine to pass back its result to the previous routine and so allow processing to take place on the way down the recursive spiral and back up it.

A general recursion

You can now appreciate why recursion can be difficult and confusing. The results you get depend very much on the type of parameter used for passing values and whether processing occurs before the recursive call or after it. A more general recursive routine is composed of a list of instructions before the recursive call and one after it

>SUB xxx(*parameter list*)
>   *list of instructions 1*
>   IF *condition* THEN CALL xxx
>   *list of instructions 2*
>END SUB

The first list of instructions will be obeyed on the way down the recursive spiral, and so will process the parameters in the same order that the copies of the routine are activated. If we assume that parameters are passed by reference then the second list of instructions processes the parameters as passed back from later activations as the spiral unwinds. For example, what does

```
SUB List(i)
i=i+1
PRINT i
IF i<5 THEN CALL List(i)
i+1
PRINT i
RETURN
```

print out after CALL List(0)? Well the argument is the same on the way down the recursive spiral, i.e. 1,2,3,4,5 will be printed, but on the way up 1 is added to the value passed back. So copy 5 receives a value of 5 to which it adds 1 to give 6, so copy 4 receives 6 to which it adds one and so on. In other words, you will see 1,2,3,4,5 followed by 6,7,8,9,10 printed on the way back up the spiral. It is in this sense that work can be performed by recursion in both directions of the spiral as long as parameters are passed by reference.

Recursion and stacks

If you perform some computation on the reverse part of the recursive spiral then the data is treated in the reverse order to the same computation done on the forward part of the recursion. In other words, recursion can be used in the same way that a LIFO stack can, to alter the order that data is dealt with. This is no accident as recursion can be thought of as a LIFO stack of procedures. Each time a new copy of the procedure is brought into existence by a recursive call you can imagine that it becomes the top of the stack so pushing all the other copies down one place. In other words the active procedure is on the top of the stack and a recursive call is just PUSH(procedure). In the same way a return from the active procedure POPs the top of the stack to make the previous procedure active. Thus a return is POP(procedure).

This description does correspond more or less to the way that recursion is actually implemented. The main difference between theory and practice is that there is no need to push and pull the text of the procedure - it doesn't

Push(procedure)

Active procedure on top of stack

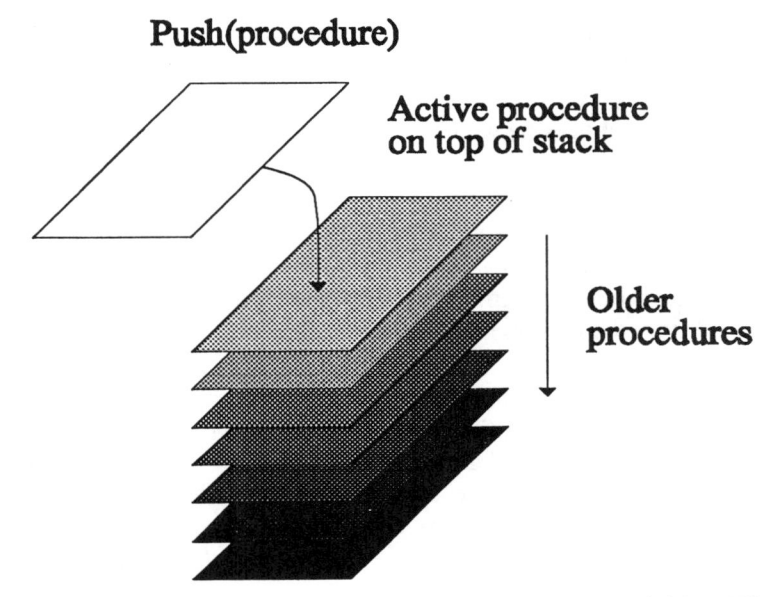

Older procedures

change, all that you have to do is push and pull the variables. Thus a recursive procedure is equivalent to a non-recursive procedure manipulating a stack of variables. Hence anything that can be done by recursion can be done using sequencing, selection and iteration plus a stack.

From another point of view this also tells us one situation in which recursion can be of use. If you need to alter the order of data you can either use a stack or recursive calls.

Tail end recursion

The simplest sort of recursion is clearly one in which everything happens on the way down the spiral. In other words one in which there are no statements after the recursive call. For example

```
SUB count(i,n)
  print i
  i=i+1
  IF i<n THEN call count(i,n)
  RETURN
```

is simple because there are no statements, apart from the obligatory RETURN, after the recursive call. The reason why this is simple is because there is only one half of the recursive spiral to worry about - everything happens on the way down and nothing happens on the way up. Indeed so little happens on the way up that there is no point in keeping the old copies of the routine. After all we know that on reactivation what each copy is going to do is shut down again by returning to an even earlier version. If parameters are passed by reference then we can even state that the final values of the parameters will be the values given by the routine that terminated the recursion.

Statements following the recursive call are often called the 'tail end' of the recursion and so it is fair to say that the absence of **tail end recursion** makes a routine simpler and more efficient. Notice that tail end recursion is needed if recursion is to be used to alter the order that data will be processed, but this isn't always the case. Indeed, as will be explained later, this isn't the major application of recursion and it is often possible to avoid tail end recursion by a simple rewrite.

Some languages that are particularly efficient at recursion achieve this by detecting the absence of tail end recursion and implementing it differently. In the case of a general recursion each call really does bring into existence a completely new copy of the routine - well at least all the variables used. This can use up a great deal of memory as each old copy of the routine is kept hanging around waiting to be reactivated on the way back up the spiral. If the compiler detects that there is no tail end recursion then there is no need to keep the old copies of the routine because their action on being reactivated is trivial. Instead a new set of variables is brought into being by simply reinitialising the old variables and at the end of the recursion the winding down is dispensed with. This saves the vast demands on memory that go with general recursion and makes infinite loops via recursion in languages such as Prolog possible.

The mechanics of recursion

The facts that are important about the way a recursive procedure works are

1) each recursive call brings into existence an entirely new copy of the recursive routine - complete with its own set of local variables

2) the result of a recursive call can depend on the type of parameter used to pass data to the routine

3) the most useful sort of parameter to use in recursion is call by reference (i.e. an input/output parameter) so that data can be passed down the recursive spiral and back down it

4) avoiding tail end recursion produces simpler and more efficient routines

5) if you do use tail end recursion then always remember that the old copies of the routine are reactivated in the reverse order to the one that they were created in

When to recurse

At this point you should have a good idea what recursion is all about. You should also be able to determine what is needed for a language to support recursion adequately. All that is needed is a mechanism for creating procedures complete with local variables and call by reference parameters. The language must also be able to handle recursive calls - i.e. allow a procedure that calls itself. Most modern languages provide these facilities, Pascal, Turbo BASIC, Modula-2, Ada etc. but most don't do anything about detecting tail end recursion and increasing efficiency when it is absent.

It is one thing to understand recursion but it is quite another to know when it might be useful. You could use it all the time instead of iteration but this doesn't really answer the question of when it is needed. Equally you could use recursion as an alternative to a stack whenever this data structure is needed, but it is usually clearer to use a stack explicitly. There are plenty of well known simple examples of using recursion to be found in text books, although the sad truth is that most appropriate examples are not simple.

The most often quoted examples are concerned with mathematical recursion and these are appropriate uses for program recursion when the mathematical recursion is itself appropriate. For example, the factorial of n, or n!, can be defined by

        if n<>1 then
           n!=n*(n-1)!
             else
        n!=1

and this is clearly a recursive definition because the ! symbol appears on both the defined and defining side of the definition. Translating such recursive definitions into recursive routines is generally easy and it would be churlish to look a gift horse in the mouth by going off and solving the problem non-recursively.

A suitable recursive procedure to calculate n! is

        fac(n,result)
          m=n-1
        IF n<>1   THEN CALL fac(m,result)
                    ELSE result=1
          result=result*n
        RETURN

This is a more interesting recursion than the earlier examples. Notice the way that m is used to compute n, n-1, n-2 .. 1 on the forward part of the recursive spiral and result is used to build up (n- 1)*n on the reverse part of the spiral.

However it is worth noting that many such problems have been cast in recursive form just for the purpose of being examples and an iterative definition, and thus routine, is often more appropriate. For example, an iterative definition of n! is simply

$$n!=n*(n-1)*(n-2)...1$$

which anyone can implement as a FOR loop in no time at all.

The most appropriate applications of recursion occur when the data structure that you are working on is itself recursive, for example a tree. A binary tree is a node, with a left-sub tree and a right sub-tree, or it is a terminal node. A sub-tree is simply another binary tree. You can see that this is recursive because the definition of a tree involves a tree. What never fails to amaze me is the difficulty of writing any sort of algorithm that processes trees, i.e. a tree search, without using recursion. The reason is simply that you have to remember which parts of the tree you have visited. Without recursion this involves complex book keeping about which right and left sub-trees have been searched - a nightmare in practice. If you use recursion then you can simply activate another copy of the program to search the left sub-tree and one to search the right sub-tree of each node. In this way the recursive calls automatically keep track of where you are. If you would like to see for yourself how essential recursion is try writing a simple program that visits each terminal node of a tree from left to right without recursion and then with recursion.

JSP and recursion

It would be nice if recursion could be brought into programming methods along with the other methods of control. This might at least save it from the 'experts only' tag it receives at the moment. However I have to admit that there are very few situations that arise in DP where it is natural and most of the examples that I know not only use advanced data structures but have an advanced theoretical foundation such as language parsing.

Of the programming methods it is obvious that only JSP is a suitable candidate for extension to cover recursion. The reasons are that natural uses of recursion are usually linked with recursively defined data structures and only JSP examines data structures to derive program structure. A recursive data structure can be represented on a standard data structure diagram by simply using the same label on a component lower down the structure as used on one higher up the structure. For example, a binary tree would be represented as

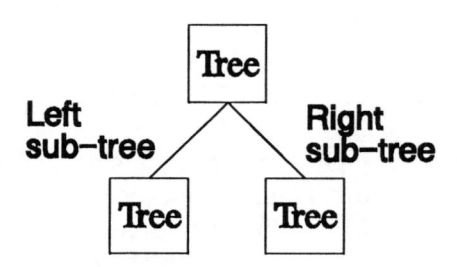

```
        Tree
       /    \
  Left      Right
  sub-tree  sub-tree
   Tree      Tree
```

It might also be a good idea to invent a special symbol to denote recursion within a data structure just to draw attention to what is going on. Once you have a recursive data structure then all that remains is to base the program structure on it in the usual way. In the case of the binary tree this produces the program structure

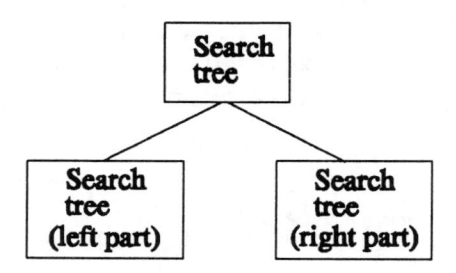

```
           Search
            tree
           /    \
    Search      Search
     tree        tree
   (left part) (right part)
```

You can see that this program structure corresponds to the recursive program

> search_tree(T)
> CALL search_tree(left(T))
> CALL search_tree(right(T))
> RETURN

Of course this doesn't include any statement that stops the recursive calls but this is easy to add. If T consists of a null tree, i.e. one that doesn't have a right and left subtree, then the recursion should stop, making the final version

JSP and recursion

```
search_tree(T)
IF T=null.tree THEN RETURN
CALL search_tree(left(T))
CALL search_tree(right(T))
RETURN
```

Of course this is just the start of a theory. For example, what constitutes a recursive structure clash and what should be done about it? Fortunately such questions haven't too much practical importance because recursion is normally used in isolation. Even if you don't want to use JSP then you should still work by the rule that the structure of the recursion should always follow the structure of the recursive data.

key points

- Recursion is iteration by self reference.

- The natural 'shape' of recursive flow of control is a spiral.

- Computation can be performed on both the forward (activation) and reverse (deactivation) part of the spiral.

- Recursion can be used in place of a stack to alter the order that data is processed - but this needs tail end recursion.

- The main application of recursion is in processing recursive data structures.

- JSP can easily be extended to include recursion as a data and program structure.

Chapter Eight
In Von Neumann's grasp

Abstraction, exceptions and concurrency

The modern digital computer is the product of many people's imagination and effort, but Von Neumann is usually credited with the key idea of an addressable store used for both data and program. In addition the phrase 'Von Neumann computer' or 'Von Neumann model' has come to mean a sequential computer with a single CPU obeying one instruction after another. For all the advances in hardware, this is still the dominant type of computer and most of our programming ideas derive from it. Recently the need to go beyond this simple model of computation has become urgent as programmers seek more sophisticated methods of working and users seek better performance.

Although the connection between a limited single processor hardware design and performance is obvious, it is less clear how hardware design can affect programming concepts. Surely programming and programming languages are free of any machine limitations? After all you can invent a language without having to consider how the machine works - the worst that can happen will be that the resulting programs will be inefficient. This is true but it seems to be much more difficult to rid ourselves of the image of the way that the computer actually works. Although programming and programming languages have the licence to be as abstract as required, moving from the real machine to higher level abstract concepts is a slow but inevitable process. We need to identify which of the ideas that we use are entirely an artifact of the underlying hardware and which are the central and machine independent concepts of programming. In this chapter the past successes of abstraction and our current problems are examined.

From the machine

All of our programming concepts have their origins in the basic mechanisms of the digital computer - how could it be any other way? The progress that has been achieved over the brief history of programming has been made by developing increasingly higher level languages that move ever further from the hardware. In other words, assembly language is most closely connected with the way that a machine works and high level languages tend to hide or ignore the underlying machine. The higher the language the more the hardware is ignored!

For example, in the early days the fundamental form of the flow of control was the branch or conditional branch instruction. You could write things like BRA *loc* which would transfer control to the instruction at memory location *loc* or BEQ *loc* which would branch to *loc* only if the result of the last operation was equal to zero. A program would be built up using these fundamental commands and programmers would think in terms of jumping from point to point to achieve whatever result was desired. As time moved on, high level languages, e.g. Fortran, abstracted this idea of branching into the GOTO label command and the arithmetic IF statement.

The GOTO label command was very like the unconditional branch in that it transferred control to the point in your program marked by the label. Its big step forward was that the label had nothing to do with the memory location used to store the instruction to be jumped to - it was just a marked point in the text of your program. That is, the abstraction was to shift the location from a point in memory to a point in the text of the program. The same abstraction allowed variables to be invented. Before named variables, data was stored in regions of memory; since the introduction of named variables data has been stored in named entities that are part of the text of a program. The key idea is the use of an **abstract label**.

The arithmetic IF is a fascinating abstraction because it was almost a wrong turning. The Fortran arithmetic IF has the form

IF (*value*) *lab1*, *lab2* , *lab3*

and this transferred control to *lab1* if *value* was negative, *lab2* if it was zero and *lab3* if it was positive. You should be able to see that the arithmetic IF is a sort of composite conditional branch on negative, zero or positive. To a modern programmer this three-way switch seems an amazing contraption. To an assembly language programmer of the time it seemed much more natural. You might like to ask yourself what would have happened if this construct had been incorporated into our modern concepts of structure?

Once you have the concept of a textual label for transfers and variables, the GOTO, and the arithmetic IF, you can start to concentrate on what you use them for rather than the details of the underlying memory and branch commands. This makes the next step in the abstraction, to loops and selects, possible. This is the stage of abstraction described in Chapters Two and Three.

Once you realise that the loop is a more appropriate concept than the transfer instructions that make it up, you start to search for other ways of writing it. In particular if you try to eliminate the idea of transfer of control then you quickly find that you need to eliminate the use of labels as well. In the early days it was the GOTO command that was singled out for criticism but in fact it is the label that is the problem. To have to mark parts of the program's text with a label is a very crude process. A much better solution is to design the syntax of the language so that the forms of control can be implemented without any direct reference to a named point in the text. So in a more advanced language the GOTO can be dispensed with in favour of a label-less method of constructing loops and selections. For example, as explained in Chapters One and Two you might write

        DO
            list of instructions
        LOOP

Notice here that the loop is contained by the bracketing keywords DO and LOOP and there is no need to label any part of the program. This has the advantage that the structure of the program can be checked automatically. That is, it is easy to spot an incorrectly formed loop using DO-LOOP but almost impossible using the GOTO *xxx* form.

In the same way labels in the program text can be removed from the select by using something like the well known block IF command

>IF *condition* THEN
>   *list 1*
>ELSE
>   *list 2*
>END IF

to mean do one of *list 1* or *list 2* depending on the truth of the *condition*. This now seems so obvious to us that it is difficult to see why any other way of doing things existed. The sad fact is that this construct is not so obvious and there were a number of mistakes on the way to it. For example, it wasn't clear that an explicit ending statement like END IF was necessary. Languages such as Pascal avoided the need for END IF by allowing only a single instruction following the ELSE. If you wanted to use more than one instruction then they had to be grouped together between BEGIN and END into a compound statement which was treated as a single statement. The problem with this approach was explained in Chapter Two as the part of the discussion of nested IFs but in short it leads to ambiguous meaning when IFs are nested, due to the difficulty of detecting when an IF statement has ended.

It is often said that the advantage of these forms is that they avoid the use of the GOTO. This is true but another way of looking at this is that they avoid the use of labels to mark locations within the text of the program. This avoidance of labels is a more general principle than just the elimination of the GOTO and perhaps the battle cry of the structured programming revolution should have been that labels, rather, than the GOTO, are evil. (In either case the battle cries are hopeless trivialisations of the real idea.)

The last relic - the interrupt

The first great abstraction in programming was the label - used for control and data structures. The second great abstraction was getting rid of the label from control structures by using more sophisticated language forms. The question that remains to be answered is whether there are any more hardware-derived concepts being used in programming that should be replaced by more abstract notions? I think that the answer is yes and this hardware concept is currently confusing the issue in a number of different areas of advanced computing. The culprit is the humble **interrupt**, without which our current computer hardware would be severely limited.

Our programming handling of the interrupt remains as primitive and as hardware-bound as it ever was. One reason for this is that high level languages have tended to abandon the whole idea of interrupts rather than attempt to find a non-machine oriented way of incorporating them. This has resulted in an entire generation of programmers missing out on the interrupt idea apart from the few who venture into the hardware and assembly language. From this point of view it looks reasonable that the interrupt should remain forever buried in our machines. There are a number of good reasons why we should turn our attention towards this relic of former times, but the most important is that it is being reintroduced into programming under the new names **events** and **exceptions**. In addition interrupts are a possible gateway to our better understanding of concurrent programming.

Hard interrupts

Before moving on to consider possible abstractions of the interrupt it is worth examining the existing hardware-based concepts. The basic idea of a processor reading instructions from memory and obeying them one after another is simple enough and powerful but it doesn't quite offer all of the behaviour that we would like. The missing behaviour is the ability to change what the processor is doing depending on conditions in the outside world. For example, if a processor spends most of its time running a program that controls a nuclear reactor then it might be nice if it could take some action on detecting something overheating.

At this point it would be easy to say that the obvious way of doing this is to invent the interrupt - but I don't think that this is quite true. You can handle this situation with an interrupt but you could also use alternative methods based on **polling**. An interrupt is a signal on a control line that forces the processor to perform a branch operation. Interrupts differ from machine to machine in how the destination of the branch is specified and in exactly when the branch is performed, but these are minor differences. For example, some machines will always branch to a fixed location on receiving an interrupt and others allow the source of the interrupt to specify it. Nearly all processors will finish the current instruction before breaking off and obeying the interrupt but there is no reason why a partially completed instruction cannot be interrupted.

Using an interrupt it is obvious how the overheating problem would be solved. An interrupt line would be allocated to the temperature sensor and an interrupt routine that dealt with the overheating would be written. If an overheat occurred then the processor would immediately, well almost immediately, jump to the **interrupt service routine**.

This is fine but it ignores the question of what happens when the interrupt service routine comes to an end. Clearly it is desirable that the interrupted program should continue from where it left off - otherwise it isn't so much interrupted as terminated! To make this possible it is necessary to store the address of the interrupted instruction and possibly the contents of all of the machine's registers. This is because the interrupt routine is almost certain to make use of the registers to do something and so their contents have to be preserved for the interrupted routine to be able to continue where it left off. In the same way you can imagine that the interrupt service routine might well have variables of its own that need preserving for use the next time it is activated.

Different machines provide different levels of protection for the interrupted routine. Many save all of the registers automatically; some (the ancient Z80 for example) provide a complete alternative set of registers for the interrupting routine to use; and some do nothing at all, leaving it up to the interrupt routine to save whatever registers it wants to use. Similarly return from interrupt instructions vary in what saved data they restore to the registers. The reason for this variation is that saving and restoring data takes time and as will become obvious, the speed of an interrupt is often the main priority.

There are other technical details of an interrupt that have to be considered if you are writing an assembly language program for real. For example, what happens if the interrupt routine is interrupted. What happens if more than one interrupt occurs at a time and what is the maximum number of clock pulses before an interrupt will be obeyed. Interrupt systems can become remarkably complex and often involve interrupt priorities, automatic masking (i.e. turning off) interrupts etc.. Even so, the basic idea is still that of an external signal transferring control to another point in the program.

You can formalise the idea of an interrupt as

1) save interrupted routine's environment
2) transfer control to interrupt routine and its environment
3) restore interrupted routine's environment and return control at the point of interrupt

Also notice that the relationship between the interrupted and interrupting routine isn't entirely equal. In particular, other interrupts ignored, the interrupt routine always starts at the beginning and finishes its job whereas the interrupted routine is started and stopped as the need arises.

Why interrupt?

Now that you know a little about interrupts you might like to ask yourself the question when are they necessary? Consider the problem of reading data in from an external device. The interrupt solution to this problem is to provide a control line that the device can use to interrupt the processor when it has data ready to be read. The processor can be getting on with some other job or task until the device interrupts and transfers control to the interrupt routine which deals with reading the data in.

The alternative approach is often referred to as polling. In this method the processor executes a loop which continually checks to see if there was any data

DO
    IF *data ready to read* THEN *read data*
LOOP

Clearly, using polling the processor is tied up with the task of reading data in from the device and cannot do anything else. This illustrates one of the reasons for using interrupt control. If there is more than one task that the processor can get on with, i.e. if you have a multi-tasking or even multi-user system, then interrupts can free the processor from wasting time waiting for external events. As external events usually take a long time in terms of the processor's time scale, this is often a useful technique.

Suppose you are not in a multi-tasking system - then what advantage does interrupt control have? Clearly as there is nothing else for the processor to do it might as well wait for the device to provide some data for it to read. In this case polling is simpler and more reliable.

However not all uses of interrupt control are involved with multi-tasking. Consider the overheating problem. How could this be dealt with by polling? You could include explicit tests for overheating at regular points in your program but it would be a difficult job to ensure that the overheating condition was checked for at short enough intervals. In this case it is much easier to deal with the overheating condition via an interrupt.

So to summarise, interrupts are useful when

1) the time spent waiting for an external device can be used for some other task

2) the time to respond to some external condition is critical

It is also important to realise that the use of interrupts is unlikely to increase the maximum rate of data transfer. That interrupts are a fast form of I/O is a common misconception. The time taken to service an interrupt is usually greater than the time taken to go around a carefully written polling loop. Interrupts are not about transferring large quantities of data at the highest possible speed but about responding as quickly as possible to occasional, and hopefully rare, external events.

Interrupts are hard

The basic idea of an interrupt is simple but their use often produces the most complex and difficult to solve programming bugs possible. The reason for this unpleasant side to interrupts comes from their asynchronous nature and their tendency to have unwanted side effects.

Interrupts are different because they can cause a transfer of control at any point in your program. It is almost as if there was an implied conditional branch to the interrupt routine after each instruction in your program. At any moment your program might stop what it is doing and jump off to some far distant point in response to an interrupt. The interrupt routine may then do a very complicated job before returning to your program. In theory the interrupt routine should do nothing to affect the running of the original program when it resumes, but then that's theory. In practice it is very difficult to ensure that the interrupt routine and the interrupted routine don't interact in unforeseen ways. The reason is that they share the resources of the same machine and so interaction is very likely and difficult to control. It is difficult if there is only one source of interrupts and one interrupt routine. It becomes a more or less impossible situation with multiple interrupts! This situation is so serious that when the Royal Signals and Radar Establishment (RSRE) Malvern decided to build a provably correct processor, VIPER, for critical applications they omitted the interrupt facility from the hardware.

In addition it is sometimes not even desirable to keep the interrupting and interrupted routine isolated. Like subroutines they often need to communicate data and results, but currently there is no sensible way for them to do this. The most usual method is to allocate shared areas of memory but this is far from foolproof.

If keeping bugs out of an interrupt system is difficult then finding them is a nightmare. The main program can be interrupted at any point and so the visible effect of any bug will change according to exactly when, and so where, the interrupt occurs. It may even be that the bug is only visible when the main program is in a particular state and so it will appear and disappear. Because of this many interrupt-related bugs are initially diagnosed as hardware faults!

Exceptions

High level languages have more or less ignored the interrupt, or at best provided facilities that are almost identical to the hardware mechanism described. Although they have ignored hardware interrupts they have introduced related methods to deal with certain types of error.

The hardware interrupt is a way of making a machine respond to an external condition within some minimum time but the same basic mechanism has also been used to deal with situations that arise within the machine and indeed within the software. For example, if you ask a machine to divide a value by zero then this will produce an error. Most machines treat this as such a serious error that they usually perform an immediate transfer to some predetermined location. This is called a **trap** or a machine **exception**. Traditionally the action that always follows a trap or exception is to abort the program. This is an example of aggressive error handling!

The trap or exception approach to errors has been adopted by most system software including compilers. At the worst they have also adopted the approach of aborting the program but some languages have provided instructions to allow the program to deal with the problem. That is when an error condition arises, or in the jargon when an **exception is raised**, the machine executes a direct transfer to an exception handler. These facilities are of course equivalent to interrupt handlers.

In PL/1 and BASIC interrupt service routines can be defined using very similar methods. In PL/1 you would write
> ON *condition* BEGIN *instructions* END;

where *instructions* constitute the interrupt service routine and *condition* is one of a number of predetermined interrupt sources such as OVERFLOW, ZERODIVIDE, KEY etc.. In BASIC you would write
> ON *condition* GOSUB *xxx*

where *xxx* is a subroutine that is treated as the interrupt routine. Neither PL/1 nor BASIC have the facility to handle interrupts above and beyond the few supplied. In other words it would be difficult to extend them to deal with specific hardware generated interrupts.

Exceptions 169

The Ada approach is very similar to that of PL/1 and BASIC but it recognises the hierarchical structure of a program to vary the interrupt handler used according to the current position within the program. The Ada exception is defined as part of a module as in

>BEGIN
>   *instructions*
>EXCEPTION
>   WHEN *condition* => *instructions* ;
>   WHEN *condition* => *instructions* ;
>   . . .
>END;

where *condition* names a particular type of exception OVERFLOW etc.. There is also a catch-all clause WHEN OTHERS that will handle any exceptions not explicitly named. If an exception occurs while the module is being executed then control will be passed to the instructions following the appropriate WHEN clause. The module will then end normally and pass control back to the module that called it. If a module doesn't have an exception handler defined then control is passed back up the hierarchy until a module is found that does have an exception handler, which is then used accordingly. The exception conditions are predefined by Ada but any module can raise a user defined exception at any time by using the command RAISE *exception-name.*

You can see that the main contribution that Ada has made to the handling of exceptions is the concept of **propagating the exception** back up the hierarchy allowing recovery methods to be used to continue a program in a reasonable fashion. Whether you feel that this is the right way to cope with the problem depends on your attitude towards the idea that a hierarchical structure which works in unexceptional circumstances is inappropriate in exceptional circumstances. It certainly solves the problem of digging your way out of a hierarchy when something has gone wrong. Without propagating exceptions this usually involves a great many tests and returns on the state of an error flag. It is interesting to ask if it is reasonable to make the normal method of stopping a program, e.g. at the user's request to Quit, the raising of an exception. If this is unhandled it then propagates back to the highest level module where the program can be safely stopped. In other words is stopping an exception or is it something that should be handled by normal program behaviour?

Concurrency

Although they provide little support for the interrupt, modern languages do provide facilities for concurrent execution of modules. For example, in Occam you can simply write

> PAR
> *mod1*
> *mod2*

to start mod1 and mod2 running at the same time. If two processors are available then mod1 will be allocated to one and mod2 to the other. If not enough processors are available then it is up to the operating system to use standard multi-tasking methods to share the processors between the modules. Ada allows concurrent execution by defining a special type of module called a **task**. All tasks declared within a procedure are started concurrently when the procedure is called.

Mechanisms for starting modules concurrently are not difficult to think up. What is difficult is controlling their interaction. The classical method is to allow concurrent modules to share global variables. This is dangerous because of the possibility of simultaneous update by both modules. Various methods have been proposed to make sure that this cannot happen. For example, a **semaphore** is a type of flag variable that can be tested and set in one operation, so avoiding the problem of simultaneous update. Once you have a semaphore you can use it to restrict access to shared variables to one module at any given time.

Ada essentially uses these ideas to implement a type of interaction called a **rendezvous**. A rendezvous between two tasks involves an entry call and an accept statement. For example, if a task contains the instructions

> ACCEPT entry1(*parameters*) DO
>   *instructions*
> END entry1;

then it will wait at the ACCEPT statement until another task makes a call to entry1. If another task makes a call to entry1 and the task that contains it isn't at the ACCEPT then it will wait until it is. You can see that calling the entry point named in the ACCEPT acts as a way of synchronising two tasks. Once the rendezvous is made, the instructions following the ACCEPT are obeyed and data is transferred via the parameter. The instructions also form a critical region that forces the calling task to be suspended. Thus the rendezvous not only synchronises the tasks, but allows data to be exchanged safe in the knowledge that only one task is active, and so the values of the parameters cannot be changed by both tasks.

The Ada rendezvous is a good method of controlling concurrency but a more modern way of exchanging data between concurrent modules is to dispense with shared variables of any kind and use message passing instead. One module can send a message to another module which can pick up the message when it is ready. Because there is no concept of a variable name associated with a message that different modules can attempt to use at the same time, there is no need to worry about simultaneous update. A module can simply enquire if there are any messages for it and send a message to another module. If you use message passing instead of variable or parameter passing the whole problem of concurrency suddenly looks a lot easier! You can even use messages passing for synchronisation if you allow a module to wait to receive a message and to wait until a message is accepted.

Occam provides an excellent example of message passing. You can declare a named communications channel between any Occam procedures. For example

>CHAN demo

defines a channel called demo. A procedure can send a message over the channel using the command

>demo!*var*

which sends the value of the variable *var* as a message. The procedure then waits until the message is read from the channel. A procedure can wait for a message over the channel using

>demo?*var*

where the value of the message is stored in the variable *var*. Thus Occam channels serve to synchronise procedures and to pass data without the need for a critical region. However notice that in Occam the communication is one way only. This is not too much of a problem because you can always declare a second channel for information in the other direction.

Interrupts and concurrency

Apart from the Ada exception which does seem to extend the idea of an interrupt, high level languages seem stuck with implementing the idea of an externally triggered direct transfer. This is crude and leaves one with the thought that there must be something better. The biggest problem with interrupts lies in controlling their interactions. There seems to be no way of passing data between interrupted and interrupting routines without using shared global variables. This is a safer way of working with interrupts than using assembly language and relying on the basic hardware facilities. In particular a high level language implementation at least allows the routines to be treated as isolated modules.

The key difference between normal modules and interrupt modules is that normal modules are activated by one another in a synchronous fashion but interrupt modules are activated asynchronously. That is, a calling routine determines when the called routine shall be active and so can pass data to it and wait for data to be returned but an interrupted routine doesn't have the benefit of this control and so cannot organise itself to perform the data transfer. In simple terms this means that it isn't enough to simply allow an interrupt routine to have parameters because this leaves open the question of what values the parameters have at any given moment.

Of course the techniques described for concurrent programming could be used to implement asynchronous interrupt modules. Many of the situations where an interrupt is used are a way of dividing the attention of a single processor. If more than one processor is available then the interrupt routine could be implemented as a concurrent task - but this isn't true of all interrupts.

If a second processor is available then the concurrent equivalent of an interrupt service routine is simply

Interrupts and concurrency 173

```
DO
    IF interrupt THEN
        original interrupt
        service routine
    END IF
LOOP
```

This means that such interrupts can be implemented using concurrent programming complete with all its theories of how to pass data between concurrent modules. But there is an important difference - the concurrent form of the interrupt routine only performs its action when the interrupt occurs, but the interrupted routine carries on regardless. In some situations this is unimportant but in others it is a serious problem. Consider the example of responding to an over heating interrupt using this method. After the interrupt two routines would be attempting to control the same equipment!

There are two possible solutions. The first is to allow the interrupt to act as a halt line for selective processes. In other words when the interrupt occurs the first routine would be forced to halt. This seems to be just as complex and hardware-inspired as the original interrupt. The second solution is to allow the interrupt routine to selectively suspend any other concurrent routines. Controlling concurrent modules, starting, stopping and suspending them, is usually thought of as the job of the operating system and even modern high level languages ignore it - perhaps they should not. Ada provides an ABORT command that allows one task to abort itself or any other tasks but a suspend command along the same lines would make life easier.

Although we are starting to develop abstract notions of how concurrent processes should be organised using message passing this is just a small part of the problem. It is not enough that one concurrent process should be able to exchange data with another when they both agree to. It is also important that one process should be able to demand the attention of another. The only way that we know how to do this at the moment is via mechanisms that look a lot like an interrupt!

key points

- Our concepts of what programming is develop by abstraction from the basic hardware concepts used to implement our programs.

- The interrupt is one of the most clearly hardware-based concepts left in programming and raw interrupts are very error prone.

- High level languages implement interrupts more or less unchanged apart from improved isolation between the interrupt service routine and the rest of the program. They fail to provide reliable methods of communication, however.

- The Ada exception extends the concept of a direct transfer due to an interrupt to include propagation back up the hierarchy to the first procedure able to handle it.

- Concurrent processes can communicate and synchronise either using shared global variables or message passing.

- Some interrupt applications can be converted into concurrent processes but others cannot unless you allow one process to alter the state of another. This is not supported in current high level languages.

Chapter Nine
The art of testing and debugging

Most programmers think in terms of testing and debugging being separate and later stages - create program-test program-debug program - but they aren't really. All the time that you spend creating a program you are using the same analytical powers to correct errors that you would use in a more well defined test and debug operation. Most of the bugs in a program are removed very early in its life, even before they have a chance to be observed in a running program and this is how it should be. However many programmers never learn how to debug properly because most of the emphasis these days is on producing correct programs in the first place. Even when the notions of testing, debugging, correctness, provability etc. are considered, the ideas often evolve very quickly towards the abstract. In this chapter the reality of testing and debugging is considered and the abstract ideas are mentioned only when they help.

Testing - knowing its wrong

Unless actively trying to fix a problem, most programmers are confident that their program works. If they believed it contained an error, then time allowing, they would have changed it. And yet programs fail all too often and the question is why? Many of the ideas described earlier in this book were introduced to try to improve the reliability of programs by making the whole process easier and less muddled. If you use structured modular programming then you are doing a great deal to ensure that mistakes are kept at bay and that when they do happen they should be easier to find.

Even so this is not enough. It is not enough to assume that a program is working. It must be tested to demonstrate that, to a reasonable degree of certainty, it doesn't fail.

Testing is a process of finding inputs to a program that make it fail. Notice that the emphasis here is on *making* a program fail. In science an experiment is conducted in an attempt to disprove a theory that is held to be true, and not to prove it. It is usually possible to find any number of experiments that will confirm a theory. The skill is generally in finding the exceptions that show the theory to be false. So it is with program testing. In the arms of a considerate tester, usually the producer of the program, even the most inadequate specimen will perform at least some tricks. Testing should be aggressive and, if you are serious about producing a good program, you should spend as much energy on finding tests that make your program fail as you did on building it in the first place.

I admit that it is difficult to summon up that much aggression towards something that you have been personally involved in and so it is common and correct wisdom that testing should ideally be performed by another programmer. A copy of a program handed to another programmer to test is usually referred to as an **alpha test** version. When sufficient bugs have been removed a **beta test** version can be handed out to selected users for field trials.

When to test?

There are two broad testing strategies - **bottom up** and **top down**. If you are using a modular method of program construction then you could test each module as it is finished and then put the whole program together. If your module specifications are correct and they produce no side effects then the finished program made of tested modules should work. Of course in the real world the finished program doesn't work for a variety of reasons. The alternative approach is leave final testing of the component modules until the entire program is assembled and then to provide test data that by its nature ensures that the correct function of each module is checked. This isn't a bad method in that it does test the finished product, but the size of the finished product often severely reduces what can be tested. There is the added problem that the component modules will only be tested as far as the finished product makes use of them. In a future revision the level of use may increase and so a module that was thought of as being perfect will be discovered to be flawed. If a module is providing a general service, such as sorting, searching, a graphics task etc., then it should be tested in isolation even if this means writing a testing module to exercise it. If a module provides a specific service to other particular modules then it might as well be tested fully after the program has been assembled.

The worst part about testing in practice is that once a bug has been detected and corrected the entire test procedure should be repeated. This is called **regression testing** and it almost never happens in practice! If your program is modular then it is often argued that the repeated section of testing should relate only to that module and the modules that are directly related to it. This is reasonable, although not a provable hypothesis.

In practice most testing consists of a cross between top down and bottom up testing. The bottom up testing is generally performed as the program is being created, and is perhaps better referred to as **stepwise testing** to complement the term stepwise refinement.

Selecting test data

There are some users, and indeed some programmers, who have a happy knack of being able to crash a program without really trying hard. They often succeed simply by misunderstanding what the program is for, or how it is supposed to work, and simply type such unlikely data that the program gives up immediately. While it is true that there is an art to constructing good test data, it is also true that there is a certain amount of science as well. Ideally good test data should at least take the program down every control path in every combination. This is usually impossible, as for any reasonable sized program the number of combinations of paths is just too great. Even so you should at least attempt to use test data that takes you down every path, if not every combination of paths. You should also select test data that represents boundary or extreme cases. Typically make the task very large, null and negative if possible - but don't forget to try a few reasonable tasks as well.

Testing aids

Much of the theory of testing was developed in the days of batch processing where a set of test data could be submitted as a deck of cards as many times as required. These days many programs are interactive and a user is needed to generate test data. One possible solution to this problem is to use a **test data generator** or **simulator** that can record what a user does and play it back repeatedly. This is an attractive idea but its main drawback is that at the end of the day the testing environment isn't identical to the final production environment. Other testing aids that are useful are **static** and **dynamic analysers**. A static analyser inspects the text of your program and lists any areas where problems might occur such as sections of code that cannot be reached, variables that are never used etc.. A dynamic analyser traces the flow of control of your program and can supply information on its structure. All things considered we are very poorly served in the area of computer aided testing.

The JL method

Once you have discovered the fact that your program contains a bug the next step it to locate it. One of the problems with discussing debugging is that there is a very powerful romantic view of the programmer as hero. The scene is very familiar

'The important program isn't working so in walks the top programmer, sleeves ready rolled up. He sits down at the desk and starts examining the fanfold listing, occasionally making marks with a fluorescent and very thick fibre tip pen. Black coffee, the main aid to debugging, is occasionally poured into a mug and so the session moves on deep into the night ...'

Well if this scene is familiar I apologise in advance for some of the remarks I am about to make. The man who walks into the room isn't a top programmer. He is clearly a man who likes hard work and long nights and we all know two things about good programmers with absolute certainty - they avoid hard work whenever possible and they have better things to do with long nights.

The reason why debugging is imagined to be this strange communing with black coffee, a listing and a fibre tip pen isn't difficult to discover. It's just an extension of the '**Just Looking**' or JL method of debugging which is so successful and powerful in the early stages. We all use the JL method. When a fault is found in a program the first thing every programmer does is to just look at the listing. Usually from the nature of the bug you can tell which part of the listing has to be looked at and if you look at it long enough the bug will make itself plain.

More realistically what happens is that you read the section of the program, think about it and how it relates to the erroneous activity that the program displays, and the reason for the bug usually becomes obvious. In a sense the JL method is a reactivation of the process used in creating the program in the first place.

The JL method is incredibly powerful and it works in most cases. This is partly a reflection of the fact that the majority of bugs are due to silly little mistakes, inconsistencies or just sloppy thinking. Most bugs, especially early ones, are easy. It also works well due to the strange fact that observing a bug can actually improve your understanding of the program! The huge success of the JL method is the cause of its greatest weakness - overuse. The reason is simply that difficult bugs occur so infrequently that many programmers never have a chance to develop any other debugging methods and so only ever use the JL method.

Difficult bugs

You can always tell when you do have a difficult bug. Usually you look through the listing for a bit, occasionally seeing likely causes that turn out not to be the trouble or are the cause of some other, yet to be discovered, bug. You may even have some firm ideas about what is going wrong but as you track each one down it turns out to be fine. After about five or ten minutes of this looking at the program the urge to get another listing and another coffee usually strikes - this is the moment you should be watching for because it is the warning light that signals a difficult bug. If the JL method doesn't work in tens of minutes at most then the chances are that it will never work, no matter how long you wait. After this critical point much of the observable activity becomes, in the jargon of the psychologists, displacement behaviour. Getting new listings, coffee, looking up obscure facts in manuals, reading the same piece of code over and over again, backwards etc.. They all serve to fill time and give the appearance of tackling the problem!

It is always a good idea to give yourself a few minutes free thinking time preferably without taking a spurious listing. This if often difficult because many programmers trying to solve a problem just don't like to stop. However the number of times that a solution occurs to people while they are waiting for the latest printout and so staring vacantly at the fanfold curling on the floor or gazing out of a window etc. must surely prove that often the real value in getting a listing is the thinking time it gives you rather than the listing itself. Breaking concentration on a problem for a few minutes can allow the mind to make a lateral jump to a previously ignored approach. All good programmers make use of this fact by spending some time every day staring at a blank wall, out of a window or just taking a siesta!

Another favourite debugging method, that many programmers discover by accident, is to explain the problem to another person. In explaining you have to move away from the program listing and think in a different way about the problem. It can even help if the person you are explaining to isn't a programmer because then you are forced to an even more radically different level. Indeed some say that the object of your explanation doesn't even have to be animate - the waste paper bin or the photocopier are equally good listeners. On the other hand sometimes it can be useful to let another programmer look at your listing. Not because they might be a better programmer or debugger than you but because they come to the problem fresh and without the preconceived notions of how the program should work.

Active debugging

The main problem with the JL method is that it is a fairly passive activity, as is suggested by the continued reference to a listing of the programs text. There are two generations of programmers. The first group learned to program using batch systems and compilers and are used to the idea that you write down your program and examine printouts. The second learned to program using VDUs and interactive systems. The difference mainly manifests itself in the desire to work with paper or the VDU screen. If you try to debug a program from a listing then you can analyse what it does but you cannot ask any questions. On the other hand if you see debugging as a dynamic activity, involving making predictions about how your program works and then testing them, the place to be is in front of the VDU screen with your program actually running.

There are only two things that characterise the behaviour of a program - the flow of control, i.e. the next statement to be executed, and the values in the variables. If you predict the behaviour of your program, say which statement will be executed next and what the values are in all the variables, and then discover you are wrong then you have found a bug. In other words logical debugging is a matter of 'predict and compare' and the first place in the program where your prediction differs from reality is the location of the bug. Of course it could be that your prediction itself was wrong but then the question would be why? Either way you are almost certain to have found the source of the problem.

It should be fairly obvious how you can predict what a program will do. If you understand the program then you can read it through and follow the logic. However how do you check your predictions? Most of the answers to this question were invented by the very first assembly language programmers and so much of the jargon is theirs. The primary method of gathering information about what a program is doing is to stop it and look at the contents of the computer's memory and registers. In mainframe days this used to be called a **memory** or **core dump** and this was another long listing that used to be studied long into the night with a fluorescent marker pen! A core dump was often produced automatically if a batch program crashed but you could also determine particular points in the programs execution where a dump would be produced. These points were generally referred to as **breakpoints** and the whole technique of using them as **breakpointing**.

Debuggers

Even today many programming languages only offer debugging facilities that are equivalent to the age old art of breakpointing. You can set a location to reach, or a condition to satisfy for the program to stop and then display values in variables or memory locations. Most will even let you modify the contents of the displayed variables/locations although this is more a testing rather than a debugging facility.

Language interpreters are ideal for use as debuggers in that they often allow you to halt the program and ask for the contents of variables to be printed in direct mode, but it is generally up to you to discover how to use these facilities for debugging. Compilers and assemblers usually have an optional **debugger** and so how to go about debugging is usually described in the manual. These days debuggers have become much more sophisticated but are still clearly based on the idea of breakpointing. They usually allow you to set a large number of breakpoints and have features such as single step and variable dumps and so on. The most sophisticated offer a facility often referred to as '**code animation**'. Roughly speaking this means providing a number of different views of the program - for example a listing with the line being obeyed highlighted, a display of variables with their current values continually updated, a display of the subroutine structure showing how deep in the hierarchy the current instruction is, a display of the contents of the stack... Code animation is a very easy to use and powerful tool but it isn't a replacement for the predict and compare method of debugging.

The current crop of debuggers are so powerful and easy to use that I have recently come across a new phenomena. Instead of sitting and 'just looking' at a listing I have seen programmers sitting and 'just looking' at the results of a debugger animating the program on the screen! When asked what they are doing the answer is usually something along the lines of 'just looking to see if I can see the bug'. There is no doubt that code animation might make it easier to see a bug but, as in the case of looking at a listing, if it doesn't give results in a few tens of minutes then it is essential to switch to an active and logical debugging method.

Where do they come from?

There have been many attempts to pin down the source of bugs and many of today's programming methods were designed to reduce the probability of bugs. Even so, after all this effort bugs still remain - and not inconsequential bugs. The question is why?

People trying to produce perfect programs have generally concentrated on linking programming to mathematics. The reason for this is that mathematics can make logical statements (theorems) that it can prove and they remain true for ever. Now programs are logical statements so presumably we should be able to prove them 'true', i.e. bug free. This turns out to be difficult for a number of reasons but perhaps the toughest is that unlike mathematics the variables in a program *change*. For example, if you see the statement IF A=0 THEN in a program then it is clear that the truth of A=0 depends on the past history of the program and cannot be deduced by a simple reading of the program text. Even so methods for checking the accuracy of a program using logical proof have been developed. An alternative approach is typified by the language Prolog where variables never change once they have been assigned a value! How can this be I hear you ask? Well the answer is that variables are always assigned their final value and if this isn't known instantly then backtracking and recursion are used to find it before the program moves on. It is a strange way to program but once you get used to it very good.

At the moment none of the formal methods of proving a program correct work for large programs. And there are people about who say that even if they did it wouldn't be the last word in getting rid of bugs. The reason is that even if a program does exactly what it is supposed to do you may not have thought of all the things it will be required to do! This is the specification error and it is becoming more important.

Programming is a very recently invented activity and we are doing better all the time but the quality of our products still leaves a lot to be desired. So far we have tackled bugs in a roundabout way by finding methods that make programming easier, but perhaps the time is close when the problem should be tackled head-on. As our programs do more and more complicated things because programming itself is easier, so the potential for serious and subtle bugs grows. It is clear that some new ideas are needed.

The Debugger's Code

- Most bugs are simple and can be found by examining the listing and thinking logically about what your program does and how the bug could possibly arise.

- If this doesn't work within a few tens of minutes then switch to logical debugging using the predict and compare method.

- Get and learn to use the best code debugger available - your time is more valuable than their cost.

- Use the code debugger but never use it as a replacement for your own logical powers of debugging. A debugger HELPS you find a bug rather than finds bugs on its own.

- If the bug is particularly difficult then spend some time in meditation.

- If meditation doesn't help then explain your program to a suitable potted plant - human or otherwise.

- Don't be too proud to let another programmer examine your code in an effort to find a bug. Don't give them too much information about what you have found out so far - they should remain ignorant of your biases.

- Try to enjoy your bugs. When you find one concentrate on how bright you are to have found it, not how dim you were to put it there in the first place.

- Don't blame the hardware too quickly.

- Debugging is more tiring and requires more energy than programming, so never work on a problem too long. Lock it away and go and enjoy yourself.

Further Reading

The classic book on managing programmers is **The Psychology of Computer Programming** by G.M Weinberg, Van Nostrand Reinhold. You should also read **The Mythical Man-Month** by F Brooks, Addison-Wesley.

To find out more about dataflow analysis you should at least read **Structured Analysis and System Specification** by T DeMarco, Yourdon Press and **Structured Design** by L.L Constantine and E Yourdon, Prentice-Hall. An alternative is **Structured Systems analysis** by C Gane and T Sarson, Prentice Hall.

On the subject of programming style I would recommend **Software Tools in Pascal** by B.W Kernighan and P.J Plauger, Addison-Wesley and **Professional Software, Software Engineering Concepts** by H Ledgard, Addison-Wesley

If you are interested in JSP then the classic work is **Principles of Program Design** by M.A Jackson, Academic Press. The alternative approach to data structure is explained in **Logical Construction of Programs** by J.D Warnier, Van Nostrand Reinhold. The syntactic approach to program construction is explained further in **Syntax Analysis and Software Tools** by K. John Gough, Addison-Wesley.

Software testing and reliability is covered in detail in **Software Engineering** by M.L Shooman, McGraw-Hill.

Although difficult to classify in terms of its coverage, every programmer should read **Programming Pearls** and **More Programming Pearls** by Jon Bentley, Addison-Wesley.

A catalogue of books on computing published by I/O Press can be obtained from

I/O Press, FREEPOST, Richmond, North Yorkshire, DL10 4BT
Tel: 0748 850459

Index

A
Abstract data type	110
Actual parameter	50
Ada	33,36,39,52, 55,65,170
Afferent	120
Algol	36
Aliasing	54-55
Alpha test	176
Analysts	20
APL	95
Arithmetic IF	161
Array	94
Assembly language	32,34,37,160

B
Backtracking	133
Bag	98
BASIC	33-34,37,39, 47,51,94,104
BCD	86
Beta test	176
Binary	86
Binary tree	155-156
Bit string	85
Boolean	89
Bottom up	74,137
Bottom up testing	176
Boundary clash	131
BRA	4,22,30
Breakpoints	181

C
C	34,36
C FOR loop	36
Call by reference	53
Call by value	53
Cascaded IF	41
CASE	40,135
Central transformation	121
Character	89
Cobol	35
Code animation	182
Coders	20
Coercion	92
Cohesion	62
COMMON	63,65
Complexity control	46
Computer Aided Software Engineering	135
Concurrency	170
Conditional loop	24,32
Conditional recursion	145
Constantine	118
Continue	32
Coupling	62

D
Dangling ELSE	40
Data	83
Data flow	118
Data structure	93,123
Database	137
De-skilling	5,20
Debugger	182
Debugging	175
Declarative programming	116
DeMarco	118
Deque	100
Direct access file	99
DO loop	35
Double ended queue	100
Dyadic select	31
Dynamic analyser	178
Dynamic data structures	99
Dynamic variables	66

E
Efferent	120
ELSE	40
ELSEIF	40
Embedded programming	136
ENDIF	162
Entity relationship model	137
Enumerated type	90,106
Enumeration loop	31,34
Event	163
Exception	168
Exception propagation	169
Exceptions	80,163
Existence	66
Exit sense	25
Export	65
Expression	59
Extent of a variable	66

F
Factorial	154
Field	96
FIFO stack	100
Files	99

Fixed point	88	**L**	
Floating point	88	Label	160
Flow chart	134	Lay out	79
Flow of control graph	7	LIFO stack	100
FOR	11,24,34-36	Linked list	102
Formal parameter	50	Local	66
Fortran	32,35,39,63, 65,89,94,160	Local variable	48
		Logic	143
Forward reference	79	Logo	142
Fractional step	36	Loop	3,23,31,161
Functional decomposition	117	Loop exit	25
Functions	59	Loop increment	36
G		Loops	10
Gane	118	**M**	
General recursion	149	Modula-2	33,39,65
Generic units	58	Modular programming	46
Global	66	Module	65,69
Global variable	48,62	Module reuse	75
GOSUB	47	Monadic select	31
GOTO	4,22,30-31, 33,47,160-162	Multi-tasking	166
		Multiple exit points	28
Graph	102	Multiple inheritance	138
H		Multiple selects	31
Hacker	20	**N**	
Hierarchy	69,77,80	Name equivalence	104
Hood	136	Named association	55
Hypertext	79	Nested IF	39
I		Nesting	29,39
Icons	113	Network model	137
IF	8,37-39,162	Non-procedural	16
IF..THEN..ELSE	38	**O**	
Indenting	12	Object Oriented	66
Infinite recursion	143	Object Oriented Design	118
Infinity	142	Object oriented Pascal	137
Information hiding	64	Object oriented programming - see OOPs	
Inheritance	138	Occam	170
Input parameters	52	ON	168
Input/Output parameters	52	OOD	118
Integer	87	OOPs	16,47,66,84, 110,136
Interrupt	163-164		
Interrupt service routine	164	Operator expression	59
Inversion	131	Operator overloading	58
Iteration	142	Output parameters	52
J		**P**	
Jackson	123	Package	65
JL method	179	Paradox	142
JMP	4,22,30	Parallel programming	15
JSP	123,154	Parameters	49
		Pascal	28,35,38,40, 51,94-95

Perceived complexity	122	Spreadsheet programming	9,16
PL/1	168	Stack	100
Polled	164	Static analyser	178
Polymorphism	138	Static variables	66
Post-exit	27	Stepwise refinement	72
Pre-exit	27	Stepwise testing	73,177
Problem assembly	44	String	104
Problem solving	43,72	Strong typing	91
Procedural	16	Structure clash	127
Procedure	47	Structure diagram	70,123
Process	2	Structure equivalent	103
Program structure diagram	119	Structured programming	5,23,116,162
Programming method	5,115	Stubs	73
Prolog	142	Sub-range type	90
Pseudo code	127	Subroutine	47

Q

Queue	100	Sum loop	46
Quick BASIC	25,67	Syntax analysis	129
		Systems design method	115

R

T

Raising an exception	168	Tail end recursion	152
Reactivation	145	Task	170
Read ahead	132	TDMSP	116
Real	87	Test data generator	178
Real time programming	136	Testing	175
Record	96	Top down	74,137
Recursion	141	Top down testing	176
Recursive structure diagram	156	Transactional analysis	121
Regression testing	177	Transfer function	92
Regular expression	129	Transfer rate	166
Relational model	137	Transformation analysis	121
Rendezvous	170	Trap	168
Representation	83	Tree	102,155
RETURN	47	Twos complement	86
Running sum	46	Type coercion	92

S

U

Sarson	118	UNTIL	25,33
Scope	66		

V

Selection	3,37,40	Variable	160
Self reference	142	VIPER	167
Semaphore	170	Von Neumann	15,159
Sequencing	3,29		

W

Sequential file	99,126	Warnier	123
Sequential IF	41	WHILE	25,33
Set	98	WIMP	113
Seven	122		

Y

Short term memory	122	Yourdon	118
Side effects	48		
Software components	75		
Software engineering	115		
Spaghetti	22		